A. J. KIESLING

WHERE
Have All the
GOOD MEN
GONE?

HARVEST HOUSE PUBLISHERS

EUGENE, OREGON

A.J. Kiesling: Published in association with the Books & Such Literary Agency, 52 Mission Circle, Suite 122, PMB 170, Santa Rosa, CA 95409-5370, www.booksandsuch.biz.

Cover photo © Andrzej Burak / iStockphoto

Cover by Abris, Veneta, Oregon

All names and anecdotal respondents throughout the book have been changed.

WHERE HAVE ALL THE GOOD MEN GONE?
Copyright © 2008 by A.J. Kiesling
Published by Harvest House Publishers
Eugene, Oregon 97402
www.harvesthousepublishers.com

Library of Congress Cataloging-in-Publication Data
Kiesling, Angela.
Where have all the good men gone? / A.J. Kiesling
p. cm.
Includes bibliographical references.
ISBN-13: 978-0-7369-2063-6 (pbk.)
ISBN-10: 0-7369-2063-3 (pbk.)
1. Mate selection—Religious aspects—Christianity. 2. Marriage—Religious aspects—Christianity. I. Title.
BV835.K535 2008
248.8'4—dc22
2007030385

Printed in the United States of America

08 09 10 11 12 13 14 15 16 / VP-SK / 11 10 9 8 7 6 5 4 3 2 1

For Kate and Emily

My biggest thanks go to the 120 singles who responded to my survey, providing the backbone of this book. Your vulnerability and raw honesty tell the true story of being Christian *and* single in the 21st century better than I ever could.

A special thanks goes to Dr. Cara Whedbee and Pastor Brad Goad for their insights and expertise on Christian singles.

contents

PART 1

I DIDN'T SIGN UP FOR THIS!

1

WHY IS IT SO HARD
TO GET MARRIED?

In the story *The Emperor's New Clothes,* everyone ignores what they can plainly see—the emperor's shocking nakedness—because groupthink encourages them to believe what they've been told versus what they know to be true. Sometimes it feels like the same thing is happening among Christian singles in our postmodern society. We're told that singleness is a special season of grace from God, a time to be devoted solely to spiritual matters, a time to have fun before we become weighed down by the responsibilities of marriage and children. Yet privately, many (if not most) singles long to find "the one." They're growing tired of the endless round of group activities as the years tick by. Everyone is supposed to be happy-happy-happy, enjoying the carefree days of singleness, but like the awkward specter of the emperor's nakedness, the unspoken truth hangs in the air: Most of us want to get married and enjoy loving, committed relationships.

At a meeting of my singles' Bible study one night, the topic turned, awkwardly, to marriage and the frustrations of singleness. As usual whenever we discussed this subject, it was a woman—in this case, me—who initiated the change in conversation.

"Why do you think it's so hard to get married today?" I asked.

Several other women nodded, suddenly keenly interested. A couple of the guys sank deeper into the sofa or fidgeted on their chairs.

"What do you mean?" a man in the group replied, a genuine look of incredulity on his face. "People get married every day. They fly off to Vegas and get married at the drop of a hat. I think our culture makes it too easy to get married. It's not treated seriously anymore."

He had a point, but it wasn't what I was driving at.

"What I mean to say is why is it so hard to *get* married?" I explained. "Look at us—15 men and women of marriageable age, all wanting to find a mate, yet nobody is getting together, and each of us is waiting for 'the one.' Why can't we find someone to marry?"

Ultimately it proved to be almost a rhetorical question, though that wasn't my intent, but the asking launched a firestorm of opinions for the next 45 minutes. This question didn't pop randomly into my head that evening. It was something I'd been mulling over for quite some time. At the singles' functions I attended, I couldn't help but notice how many attractive women milled around, trying to be sociable and likable, and most of all, trying to get noticed. The guys were there too, of course, but generally ran fewer in number—sometimes as little as one man to every four or five women. What struck me, however, was that these weekly gatherings (in this case, at a large church) gradually began to seem like the last place in the world to meet someone interesting of the opposite sex. Some people were what I call "lifers," longtime members of the church's singles' group who had been hanging around literally for years, making friends, going to all the functions, getting to know just about everybody, but oddly enough, they were still single. Others, like me, attended the group and its multitude of functions for two years or so before finally giving up in frustration, opting to attend a small-group singles' Bible study instead.

Welcome to the Twilight Zone

In conversations with some of my single girlfriends, we joke that being single and Christian in a postmodern world is like living in the Twilight Zone. We bolster each other with our humor, wisecracking and telling first-date horror stories about our ventures into the netherworld of online dating, but sometimes the reality of *living* in this odd parallel universe is anything but funny. I should know. Single-again for ten years now, I've experienced the loneliness so deep it feels like a physical pain, as well as the giddy expectation of meeting someone new—someone promising (could he be "the one"?)—only to be disappointed yet again and struggling to fit in at social functions where everyone, it seems, is part of a couple but you.

And then there's the weirdness of getting back "out there" after years of being "off the market," so to speak. Crass as it sounds, there really is a lot of truth to the whole market mind-set, and you find that out fast once you enter this subterranean world of commodity shoppers—especially now that finding someone to date online has become mainstream, no longer a recourse only for the bolder among us. I read a headline on Yahoo the other day that stated one in six married couples now meet each other online, but not too long ago, online dating was still the anomaly, and scary enough to conjure images most single women try not to think about.

So now we've become accustomed to meeting people over an electronic connection, e-mailing back and forth after we choose a photo we like and read a few descriptions about the person that may or may not be true. My own experience followed the usual pattern. I was hesitant at first, then eager as the stories floated around about so-and-so meeting her husband online, and the guy at work who found someone special on the Web after years of not dating. It was easy to fall into the expectation game. At first I was overwhelmed and flattered by the influx of male attention. It's quite gratifying to come home and find that 15 men have e-mailed you, and 5 have sent you a digital wink. *Hmm, maybe this online thing isn't so bad after all,* I thought. But my enthusiasm waned after I started actually meeting these men in person. I played by all the safety rules—meeting only in public places over coffee or lunch; driving myself there and back home again; never, ever getting into a car with someone I had just met.

To be fair, many of the men I met were genuinely nice guys, but when you're in your upper 30s or mid-40s and beyond—how shall I say it?—life just has a way of piling the baggage on. And those are the ones who actually look like their photos. I remember Tom, whom I clicked with immediately and found myself attracted to. *This is someone I could enjoy getting to know,* I was thinking as a waitress set our sandwiches in front of us at the restaurant where we met. As we talked, however, Tom mentioned something about his ex-wives. *No matter,* I reasoned. *It's rare to find someone who hasn't been married at least once or twice these days.* But when I offered, "So you've been married twice before?" he responded, "No, three times." So help me, I blanched, even though I tried desperately not to. And in that split second of fate, I wondered, *What am I going to be, ex-wife number four?*

Then there was Greg, who was posing as a Christian but had a secret agenda of getting me—or any woman presumably—into bed. Jim kind of grossed me out in person; Bob was still in love with his ex-wife; and Steven (an overwhelmed single dad) was shopping for a mother for his two young children. Attractive and a fellow music lover, Steven bantered easily and won me over by his charm. Yet I was busy raising my own two teenage daughters and thought honestly, *Am I up for this? Starting all over again with two young ones who aren't my own children?* If that was in God's plan for me, then yes. But before I could even think that far, Steven correctly ascertained that I was just a couple of years from the empty-nest phase and probably not the best candidate for his mommy position.

We parted company in the parking lot. By this point all of his charm had shut down, and he made a beeline for his car, walking a few strides ahead of me. He turned back toward me at the last minute and extended his hand. "It was very nice chatting with you," he said, then he turned on his heel and left.

It felt like an interview for a job—one I had failed to get.

To all of those happily married people out there who met their spouses online, I hope you won't be offended by these stories. Consider them the tongue-in-cheek (although true) anecdotes of a hapless single woman living in metropolitan America. As I said, these tales from the front lines make for good laugh sessions with girlfriends or lively entertainment for family members at holiday gatherings, yet beneath all the laughter and eye-rolling, I find myself growing disillusioned by degrees. My thoughts go something like this: *Do I really want my love story to be, "Well, there was this Web site, and he saw my photo and I saw his, and then he e-mailed me…"?*

The happy couples who do end up together after an online match don't seem bothered by the lack of mystery at the outset. Somehow, though, I think I was born one of those who must have mystery and romance and longing and, finally, longing fulfilled. I sit in darkened theaters watching the latest remake of a Jane Austen classic, and my eyes well up with tears. Call me odd perhaps, but as you'll soon discover, there's a whole subculture of postmodern women like me who can't quite reconcile the flat, perfunctory nature of modern dating with the bittersweet tension of romances from an earlier era that we read about in books or watch on-screen. We long for something more, and fortunately, many of the guys out there do too.

Our challenge, then, is actually *finding* someone to marry and stemming the tide of a culture gone awry. As it turns out, finding each other may be the easy part. Altering who and what we've become—and understanding how the culture has changed both the inner and outer landscape of single adulthood—may prove to be the real obstacle.

Culture Wars

Certainly I'm not the first to notice the difficulty today's singles have making long-lasting commitments, much less finding the one they want to spend the rest of their lives with (if we're even capable of such a commitment). Nor am I the first to write a book about it. In *Unhooked Generation: The Truth About Why We're Still Single,* author Jillian Straus relates how she first became aware of this social pandemic.

At age 30, after multiple phone conversations with her male and female friends, she couldn't help noticing that the topic of [their] failing relationships dominated almost every conversation. Though they lived in different parts of the country, came from different kinds of families, and worked in different professions, so many of them were echoing the same sentiment: They were frustrated, confused, and even depressed about their romantic lives. Some had turned to their parents for guidance. But the older generation, no matter how sympathetic, didn't seem to truly understand their plight…It was as if the two generations were speaking a different language.[1]

Eventually Straus interviewed 100 singles from six cities in different geographic locations, focusing on middle- and upper-middle-class individuals "because these were the people who had the same questions I did." As she talked with them, over and over again they said it was hard to meet other singles because of where they lived. "In other words," Straus writes, "I saw crowds of people all looking for someone special—all unable to find what they were looking for, and all convinced the problem was where they lived. It was clear to me that geography was not the problem, however—the problem had something to do with the seeker's approach."[2]

We Are What We've Become

Ultimately Straus concludes that it isn't anyone's imagination; it *is* harder to find lasting love in today's society, and she identifies seven "evil influences" that have changed us from the inside out: a self-serving, "What's in it for me?" culture; a multiple-choice culture; the effects of divorce; the feminism fallout; a "Why suffer?" mentality; the celebrity standard; and delayed marriage. Before I even stumbled across Straus' book, many of these themes had already cropped up in the responses I culled from my own research and general observations, but I highly recommend her book to anyone wanting to delve deeper into this topic.

It's hard to ignore the validity of these influences. As you read through the survey responses of single men and women in this book, you'll hear these same themes, often worded in different ways and using different monikers, but still there all the same. The real questions that emerge in the wake of groundbreaking books like Straus' are, Why a book about Christian singles? Why break out this subset of singles from the larger culture and focus an entire book on their struggles to find mates? The answer is simple: *Because Christian singles, although a subset of the singles culture as a whole, are supposed to be a very different subset, viewing marriage as a positive thing, God's original design for meeting our needs for intimacy and romance.* Unlike our non-Christian cohorts, in our search for soul mates, we're not supposed to embrace the overwhelmingly pervasive trends of living together out of wedlock, casual "hookups," or reckless serial monogamy, leaving a trail of broken hearts in our wake (and sometimes having our own hearts broken in the process).

Yet looking around at the surplus of singles in the church—some hopeful, some desperate, some mildly bored, others depressed or even despairing—it's plain to see that all is not right in Christendom. Somehow we've taken what was meant to be a very natural process (boy meets girl, boy woos girl, boy marries girl) and turned it into what can seem at times a virtual impossibility. And here I'm referring to the never-married single population. What goes on with the single-again group is another thing altogether and has its own unique set of obstacles.

The truth, of course, is that while we Christian singles are a subset of society, we're more influenced by our culture than we may think. In a very real sense, Christians have always been at war with the culture they live in, and we fight against a strong opponent. I suspect contemporary Christian singles are reaping the harvest of decades' worth of seeds sown askew in the culture at large. The sexual revolution, the women's liberation movement, women pouring into the workforce, a generation of children growing up in day-care centers, the powerful influence of entertainment media in a sexualized culture, mind-boggling divorce statistics, cohabitation replacing the marriage covenant—all of these influences and more have combined to change the way men and women interact with one another, and we Christians aren't exempt from the fallout.

One single man—in his early 30s, never married, and a virgin—voiced his concern about negative societal influences, saying, "*Christian dating scene* seems like an oxymoron in this society. It isn't that I don't believe in dating; I just don't believe in dating by the current social norms. The way things are now, people just seem to use each other. There's no giving to a relationship, just dating to see what one can get out of it sexually, socially, emotionally, etc. It's very selfish, and I refuse to play the game."

A single woman democratically laid the blame for what I call the "marriage crisis" in the church at the feet of both men and women—and the impossibly high standards we often set for ourselves: "We're a generation that wants guarantees and good return policies. We're afraid to make the same mistakes our parents did, and therefore we want everything to be perfect before we get married. We want a trial period (hence the living-together epidemic), but we're missing the point big time!"

"We've lost sight of what's important in life, which translates to what's important in a mate," wrote a woman who has been married twice and is now single again in her mid-40s. "We sabotage ourselves by being heavily influenced by the mass bombardment from the media. You must be [FILL IN THE BLANK] to be desirable or loved or accepted. We can't even think for ourselves anymore."

"Both sexes, as well as societal and cultural influences, are to blame," wrote a woman in her 40s who has never married. "Not to mention the breakdown of the family and the lack of healthy, positive role models. I would also say that within the church the proliferation of singles groups is to blame. Creating inauthentic communities based almost solely on marital status (not age, as many singles groups range in age from the low 20s to the mid-40s) fosters and causes unhealthy and immature emotional and social tendencies to fester and doesn't allow people (married or unmarried) to grow and learn from people in different stages of life. Singles can learn by seeing a healthy, loving, stable marriage lived out in the lives of others in the church. And marrieds can learn that singles are grown-ups too!"

A single man in his 50s took a more philosophical view of the problem: "There are no longer serious cultural demands that we be married. There is no longer a financial necessity to get married. People in the developed world no longer know how to choose to be happy with a partner because they don't have to."

A woman in her late 30s graciously offered the opinion that we can't blame the opposite sex for the marriage crisis in the church: "I think it's a much more complex issue, which involves the lifestyle we adopt, the society we live in, and its effects on the traditional-family model and gender expectations."

Clearly, we're a generation of Christian men and women who find ourselves paddling upstream in a stiff cultural current. The frustrations I myself encountered being single and Christian in an "evil generation" (to use biblical language) seemed to be the common lot of so many of my peers. I went in search of answers, not to try to solve the big cultural-shift types of problems cited earlier, but to hear from real singles who professed faith in Christ, yet found themselves single, despite their wishes to the contrary. My search ultimately led me to conduct an online survey, which we'll look at in depth in the next chapter.

Do you think you know what makes that single guy or gal across the room tick? You may be surprised!

THE SURVEY—WHAT SINGLE MEN AND WOMEN REALLY THINK

At first I planned to target only Christian women in my survey, but soon it became clear that this was an issue both genders are passionate—and perplexed—about, though women are the most vocal. I logged on to Christian-singles forums across the Internet, putting out the word about a survey I created for real-world single Christian men and women. The responses trickled in at first but then gained momentum. Ages ranged from the 25 to 30 category to 50-plus. The survey did not pinpoint the specific regions of the country these singles lived in, but the nature of the Internet—affording communication without geographical boundaries—offers a built-in spectrum of respondents.

That said, let's dig into the survey results. (For the sake of simplicity, any reference to singles or the issues they deal with applies to *Christian* singles unless specifically stated otherwise.)

Longing for Love

Out of 120 random Christian singles surveyed for the book (see actual survey at the end of this chapter), not one man or woman responded no to the question, "Do you want to be married someday?" A total of 72 percent answered yes, with 20 percent claiming, "If I meet the right person," and 8 percent saying, "Not sure." Overwhelmingly, the majority of singles who responded to the survey had never been married (71 percent) and had been single an average of one to five years past the age of 25 (43 percent). But this was only part of the social landscape, and the numbers proved it. You only have to drop by any Christian singles gathering to realize that this subculture is rife with men and women who are back "on the market" in the aftermath of divorce, and sometimes multiple divorces. Sure enough, they showed up on the survey results, but for whatever reason, they represented a much smaller percentage of respondents in this survey. (One theory is that the younger demographic—singles ages 25 to 35—are more likely to log on to Christian singles forums on sites like MySpace and Crosswalk.) Of those who had been married at one time, 13 percent said they had been married once, 4 percent had been married twice, and 1 percent had been married three or more times.

A surprising number of those who took the survey were virgins (42 percent), and most claimed they were not sexually active (45 percent), which flies in the face of the common assumption that many Christian singles are having sex as often as their non-Christian counterparts. (Only 13 percent of Christian singles in the survey claimed to be sexually active.)

As to the question, "How often do you date?" respondents were offered six multiple-choice answers:

- every week (6 percent),
- once or twice a month (11 percent),
- now and then (26 percent),
- once or twice a year (18 percent),
- "I don't remember the last time someone asked me out" (36 percent), and

- "I don't believe Christians should date" (3 percent).

When asked where they meet the people they date respondents gave one of seven multiple-choice answers, with church coming in first (27 percent), followed by friends/family (24 percent), and the Internet in third place (13 percent). Other responses included work (12 percent), clubs/organizations (8 percent), sporting activities (3 percent), singles bars (3 percent), and other venues (10 percent).

God Still Number One

We're all drawn to a particular person for very distinct reasons—from that elusive quality called chemistry to physical good looks to shared likes and dislikes. If someone could package the magic formula for what draws one man to one particular woman, and vice versa, Internet dating sites would pay millions to purchase it. Let's face it: Attraction is a tricky thing—something you can't muster up or fake—and many people claim they don't have a specific "type" when it comes to the opposite sex. They just know what they like when they see it.

Having said all that, certain patterns do emerge when you offer a limited number of response choices (15) to the question, "Which five attributes most draw you to date a particular person?" Across the board, both male and female Christian singles chose "strong faith in God" as their number one requirement (17 percent) when selecting a dating partner. A good sense of humor clocked in at second place (12 percent), followed by sharing similar interests and honesty, both at 11 percent, fun personality (8 percent), kindness (8 percent), and mutual attraction (7 percent). Good looks (5 percent), self-confidence (5 percent), and "You just click" (5 percent) tied for seventh place, trailed by financial stability (3 percent), quelling the common male belief that most women are gold diggers at heart.

"A certain sex appeal" accounted for 3 percent of the responses, whereas "the recommendation of someone you trust" drew 2 percent of the votes. "They pursued aggressively" also garnered 2 percent of the votes, followed in last place by "a quiet, serious nature" (1 percent).

Dating Deal Breakers and Marriage Makers

Next I asked singles what they considered deal breakers in a dating relationship. They were told to choose three out of seven possible answers. In descending order, here are the traits most likely to drive a potential mate away, according to survey respondents: anger problem (22 percent), emotionally unavailable (21 percent), incompatible with one's friends/family (16 percent), flirts with opposite sex (13 percent), financially unstable (12 percent), weight gain (4 percent), and a category called "other" that garnered 12 percent of responses.

The last of the hard-data survey questions asked respondents what four assets they consider most important in choosing a mate. Once again, a strong faith in God was far and away the favorite at 21 percent. Next, singles expressed the importance of someone who shares their values (20 percent), followed by someone who is responsible/dependable (15 percent). Other responses included compatibility (15 percent), a sense of humor (12 percent), wants children (7 percent), financial stability (4 percent), and good looks, which came in last at 3 percent. A category called "other" also drew 3 percent of responses.

Looking for "the One"

The survey revealed yet another surprise: More than twice as many people *don't* believe the soul-mate theory as those who do. Specifically, the question asked, "Do you believe there is only *one* person for you out there?" The results: 29 percent said yes; 71 percent said no.

In addition to answering hard-data questions about age and gender and other issues, most of the singles surveyed opted to answer two open-ended essay questions:

> 1. What would you like to tell the opposite sex about your frustrations with the Christian dating scene?

2. How do you think the opposite sex has contributed to the current "marriage crisis" (delayed marriages, no marriages, bypassing suitable mates, etc.)?

Reading through the responses to these questions revealed the depth of frustration and range of emotion these issues generate. One woman's answer seems to sum up the heart cry that led me to write this book: "I think, generally, Christian men are looking for a Martha Stewart, Mother Teresa, [and] Venus Williams in Jessica Simpson packaging. There is no meeting those standards, and in the meantime, I just get older and older."

Another woman lamented, "I could literally count on the fingers of one hand the single Christian men in my church (and I live in a capital city). Finding an eligible guy at all, not to mention the love of your life, is akin to the Holy Grail these days."

The responses from both men and women ranged from the angry ("Stop hanging out with girls and *ask* a woman on a date!") to the heartbreaking ("I especially hate it when I make an effort to be seen or recognized and no one notices. I would love to see someone interested in me. What am I doing wrong?") to the weary ("I don't have the energy anymore to address the problem.")

What Is That Guy—or Gal—Really Thinking?

In culling responses from the men and women who took the survey, clear patterns began to emerge. Themes started to bubble to the surface. The sheer volume of women's responses on one specific topic, for instance, indicated that this subject weighs more heavily on their minds than any other when it comes to their frustrations with the Christian singles scene in general and single Christian *men* in particular. After studying the data, I broke up the responses into six key frustrations for women—how single women view the Christian singles scene—and seven key frustrations for men. Yes, men's frustration responses ranged across more topics than women's, and

I briefly considered whittling their list to six to make it match the women's. But a closer look indicated that these seven issues needed to be voiced. Since fewer men responded to the survey overall than did women, their comments were weighted more heavily than those of their female cohorts.

Keep in mind that the following lists represent a broad range of issues because some responses naturally included multiple topics in a single answer, as if—finally given the chance—these men and women wanted to vent everything that's been smoldering in their minds and hearts about the Christian single life.

Women's Top Frustrations with Single Men

1. "We want to be pursued, and men won't step up to the plate!"
2. "Guys are looking for a supermodel with a Mother Teresa personality."
3. "All the good ones are taken."
4. "Men today are emotionally and spiritually immature and take too long to grow up."
5. "Men want to play the field or have their cake and eat it too."
6. "Too many Christian men try to push sexual boundaries."

In a later section of this book, we'll examine each of these six frustrations in more detail, including actual responses from the women who registered their feelings about each.

Men's Top Frustrations with Single Women

1. "Women expect too much from us (spiritually)— real men are rough around the edges."

2. "Too many women bypass nice guys in favor of 'bad boys.'"

3. "Christian women don't keep themselves attractive enough, and many are overweight."

4. "We have a very real fear of divorce."

5. "Christian women are too shallow and self-absorbed, or just want to be 'friends.'"

6. "It's hard to tell Christian women from non-Christians these days."

7. "Christian women aren't available."

As with the women's responses, we'll examine the seven top frustrations men voiced in a later section of the book, including the actual answers they wrote on the survey.

In spite of their frustrations with the opposite sex, however, both men and women agreed that one huge factor has contributed to their frustrations and their struggle to find mates: the culture we live in and how it subtly works against us.

CHRISTIAN SINGLES SURVEY

March 8, 2007–May 8, 2007

Taken via SurveyMonkey.com
(Percentages have been rounded to the nearest whole number.)

1. What is your age?	Response Percent	Response Total
25–29	30%	36
30–34	30%	36
35–39	15%	18
40–44	7%	9
45–49	12%	14
50+	6%	7
Total Respondents		120
(skipped this question)		0

2. What is your gender?	Response Percent	Response Total
Female	70%	84
Male	30%	36
Total Respondents		120
(skipped this question)		0

3. How long have you been single (past the age of 25)?	Response Percent	Response Total
1–5 Years	43%	52
6–10 Years	27%	33
11–15 Years	11%	13
16–20 Years	3%	3
20+ Years	16%	19
Total Respondents		120
(skipped this question)		0

4. Have you ever been married? If yes, how many times?*	Response Percent	Response Total
No	71%	95
Yes	11%	15
Once	13%	17
Twice	4%	5
Three	1%	1
Total Number of Responses		133
Total Respondents		120
(skipped this question)		0

* Required more than one response.

5. Do you want to be married someday?	Response Percent	Response Total
Yes	72%	86
No	0%	0
Not Sure	8%	10
If I met the right person	20%	24
Total Respondents		120
(skipped this question)		0

6. How often do you date?	Response Percent	Response Total
every week	6%	7
once or twice a month	11%	13
now and then	26%	31
once or twice a year	18%	22
I don't remember the last time	36%	43
I don't believe Christians should date	3%	4
Total Respondents		120
(skipped this question)		0

7. Where do you meet the people you date?*	Response Percent	Response Total
church	27%	72
friends/family	24%	66
Internet	13%	36
work	12%	31
clubs/organizations	8%	22
sporting activities	3%	9
singles bars	3%	7
other (please specify)	10%	27
Total Number of Responses		270
Total Respondents		119
(skipped this question)		1

* Required more than one response.

8. Are you sexually active?	Response Percent	Response Total
yes	13%	15
no	45%	54
I am a virgin	42%	51
Total Respondents		120
(skipped this question)		0

9. Which five attributes most draw you to date a particular person?*	Response Percent	Response Total
honesty	11%	67
financial stability	3%	21
good looks	5%	33
sense of humor	12%	74
strong faith in God	17%	104
mutual attraction	7%	46
fun personality	8%	51
quiet, serious nature	1%	7
recommendation of someone you trust	2%	14
you just "click"	5%	28
kindness	8%	49
self-confidence	5%	32
a certain sex appeal	3%	16
they pursued aggressively	2%	11
similar interests	11%	67
Total Number of Responses		620
Total Respondents		119
(skipped this question)		1

* Required more than one response.

10. What are deal-breakers for you in a dating relationship? *	Response Percent	Response Total
anger problems	22%	90
flirts with opposite sex	13%	52
incompatible with your friends/family	16%	63
financially unstable	12%	48
weight gain	4%	18
emotionally unavailable	21%	84
other (please specify)	12%	50
Total Number of Responses		405
Total Respondents		118
(skipped this question)		2

* Required more than one response.

11. What four assets are most important in choosing a mate?*	Response Percent	Response Total
financial stability	4%	19
compatibility	15%	72
strong faith in God	21%	106
sense of humor	12%	60
wants children	7%	36
shares same values	20%	97
good looks	3%	17
responsible/dependable	15%	76
other (please specify)	3%	14
Total Number of Responses		497
Total Respondents		119
(skipped this question)		1

* Required more than one response.

12. Do you believe there is only *one* person for you out there (soul mate)?	Response Percent	Response Total
yes	29%	35
no	71%	85
Total Respondents		120
(skipped this question)		0

A Years-Long Drought

If you believe the leading women's magazines of our time, everyone is dating—from plus-size to pint-size, plain or "hot." Our culture is obsessed with meeting the opposite sex, and if we're honest, we're probably no exception. Articles and talk shows encourage us to meet at least three new people (read: men) a month to widen our options. Has it been a few months since your last date? Well, get back out there, girl, because you won't find Mr. Right sitting home moping in front of the TV.

The first time I read such an article, I nearly gulped audibly. A few months? Try a few years. Apparently I knew a secret the magazine editors didn't: There exists a subculture of attractive, datable women—in this case, Christian women—who often haven't dated in so long, they've forgotten what it feels like to be asked out. These women want to get married but find themselves in a maddening catch-22. The pool of men they look to as potential mates—Christian males—either aren't asking or they're waiting so long to get married that when they do finally go wife hunting, they often shop in the 10-to-15-years-younger category, bypassing women around their age who are still looking for mates. Meanwhile, if a frustrated Christian woman decides to accept a date with an unbeliever, she wades into dangerous waters spiritually, emotionally, and physically—and also ignores the serious scriptural warning not to be unequally yoked with unbelievers.

My own social circle was a microcosm of this trend, so I didn't have to look far to find validation. Other than a slew of "e-dates" (dates set up from online dating sites) that went nowhere, many of the women I knew hadn't had a real date in a couple of years. By "real" date I mean the old-fashioned kind where boy meets girl face-to-face and asks her out. Meanwhile, I knew several other attractive single women in their mid-30s to mid-40s who hadn't dated in so long one called it her "years-long drought." By far the largest category of respondents in my survey (43 out of 120) said, "I don't remember the last time someone asked me out." It turns out there's a whole subculture of Christian singles who are flying under the radar of the dating world—and they're flying solo.

When the U.S. Census Bureau released its groundbreaking population statistics in 2004, the American media reported a startling fact: We have more singles than at any other time in the history of the United States. But like the saying, "Water, water everywhere, and not a drop to drink," we seem to live in an age of single surplus but have few good candidates for marriage, let alone someone to go out with. Indeed, the Census Bureau reported that 86 million singles now populate America, and the numbers are steadily climbing.

With all these singles, why aren't Christians getting married? Or more to the point, why are so many marriage-age women growing old alone?

As a writer, I've adopted a personal system that tells me when a topic warrants ink: Everywhere I go, I bump into the same issue, the same conversation, the same scenario so many times that a little voice inside says, "This one deserves a closer look." In this case, it has become painfully clear to me that the subset of Christian America has a relational crisis on its hands. A whole generation of marriageable women is growing older alone, despite their availability and desire to be married. As the years tick by and these women move into their early 30s, then mid-30s, then late 30s, and then, finally, their 40s and beyond without finding Mr. Right, despair and disillusionment set in. In fact, by the time they reach the big 4-0, many have given up on ever finding the love of their lives.

What Happened to the Fairy Tale?

In its earliest stages, the working title for this book was *The Lost Girls.* This captured the essence of the sociological trend I was trying to report on: that there exists a vast undiscovered population of single women (in this case, specifically Christian women) whom marriage seemingly sidestepped or at least put on hold for an indefinite period of time. In many ways it seems these women are truly lost in time, set apart from the generations that have gone before them. Unlike their female ancestors, these women face a culture that works against their hopes of finding a mate.

The title resonated with some people immediately, but for others it seemed to imply that this demographic of women was abandoned to a lonely fate with no hope of finding lasting love. As I did research for this book I stumbled upon the following passage by Rachel Greenwald in her New York Times listed best-selling book *Find a Husband After 35,* in a section titled "Who Moved My Altar?"

> It really is different looking for a husband after 35. It's as though someone moved your altar: You weren't supposed to be standing here. Maybe you are part of the group of women whom I call the *"Lost Cinderella Generation."* You broke the glass ceiling, but broke your glass slipper along with it.[1]

For the large number of single women in their 30s and beyond, being alone seems to be a constant reminder that they failed in the marriage game. It can also seem like the death of the fairy tale. They wonder, *Why didn't my life turn out the way I thought it would? Why didn't my prince ever show up? Has God forgotten about me? Am I unlovable? Undesirable?*

In talking to many of these women I heard and felt the frustration, loneliness, disillusionment, and despair that can often engulf a woman as the years tick by, yet the same conversations were often woven with humor, hope, and a spiritual maturity lacking in so many postmodern adults' lives.

"I Feel Like a Drowning Man…"

Take Laura, age 35, who lives in a capital city known for its intellectual population. A good place to meet single men, you'd think. That's what Laura always assumed, being both intellectual and attractive. But she has come to the conclusion that her quiet, shy demeanor makes it difficult for her to actually *meet* men—or for men to approach her. "I take part in a community group at church, and there are lots of intellectuals, pretty much everybody," she says. "Everyone I know has a great job and does interesting stuff. It seems like there are a lot of singles in this area, but it's hard to meet someone. I have a hard time just meeting *anyone*—I don't know if it's because I'm shy or what. I hear this from girlfriends. I go to a big church, look around, and there seem to be a lot of single people there. But other than one single girlfriend, I don't really know anyone there."

To add to her frustration, Laura says it seems like all the guys she might have been interested in have gotten married, or they're wondering about their sexuality, or they don't want to commit, or they've left the church. "I feel like if I weren't looking for an evangelical Christian guy, I wouldn't have a hard time meeting men—if my standards were different," she says. "I don't know if the whole sex thing is harder for them, so they just give up, or that there are more girls in the church. In my age group, there seem to be more girls. In the Christian community, there's a whole other layer of 'How do I show him I'm interested but not be too aggressive and turn him off?'"

There are times I would love to share all this with someone. At times it is a source of great pain. I guess my challenge is to believe that God is using it for good.

Laura hasn't dated much, other than a couple of guys in her 20s. One was serious, but it didn't work out. "In my 30s, I don't know if I've even been asked out," she reflects. "I've done some online dating, and I met some interesting people, but nobody I wanted to continue a relationship with." On an overseas trip she met someone who seemed to hold possibilities, but in the end, the budding relationship fizzled. "Part of me wants to say he's one of those noncommittal guys who never wants to be married, but I think he just wasn't interested enough to pursue it," she says.

When asked what she's looking for in a man, Laura told me she wants someone who loves God with all his heart and who adores her. She admits there are a lot of assumptions in that—he'll be intelligent and fun and kind, but basically he'll be completely committed to his faith and to God.

Laura said she senses a great hesitancy to commit to marriage among the single guys in the church, and most of her girlfriends agree. She adds,

> One of the things I've sensed is that our standards have become so high, we're really kind of expecting perfection. We're expecting the other person to be everything. In *Boundless* [a Webzine], I read about a guy who was going out with a girl. She was great, "really fun," he said,

but "she's not a 10." We've stopped valuing character; it's not something we respect. If you look at modern media—TV—it's about, Are you funny? Are you good in bed? Those are the things women are encouraging. If we don't expect anything else, if we don't value anything more than that, then it's not going to happen.

Whenever she feels lonely, Laura gets out of the house, calls her friends to hang out, or gets together with her family. At this point she's resigned to her fate as a single woman and told me that dating takes so much energy, it's easier just to stop. Before the interview ended, I asked her the hardest question of all: Do you feel like there's someone out there for you, someone you simply haven't met yet? Her reply:

No, I don't feel that there's someone out there for me. I would like to believe it, but at this point I don't. I don't feel any sense of security in that. My feelings go in phases. There are times I would love to share all this with someone. At times it's a source of great pain. I guess my challenge is to believe that God is using it for good. Sometimes I feel like a drowning man; oh, I want this so much! But if I ever meet someone, I'm afraid that the depths of my desire will be too much, that it'll be too much for one person to fulfill.

A Time of Our Own Making

None of this is to say that God no longer works on behalf of His "handmaidens," or that His perfect timing isn't at work among us. As a lifelong Christian, I have to believe He is working behind the scenes to draw two hearts together at just the right time. But the pragmatic side of me—the observer, the realist—can't help but wonder why our generation is so different from those that have gone before. The obvious conclusion, it seems, is that our culture wields far greater influence than we give it credit for. Let me give you an example of what I mean.

A well-meaning soul may tell a lonely single woman, "First Corinthians 7:8 says it's better to remain single. God may not want you to get married; why don't you pray about it?" But consider this: In first-century Hebrew culture, which would have included members of the early church, marriage was so much a part of the cultural norm, men and women were considered anomalies if they didn't have a spouse. Most marriages were arranged, often long before the young bride and groom reached marrying age. Indeed, matchmaking was a lucrative and necessary trade in every community.

My point is that no one seemed bent on imploring the heavens about whether to get married; marriage was a given. And except for the injunction to seek out a believing mate, the early Christians (most of whom were Jews) went about the business of marrying and giving in marriage as all other Jews did.

Centuries later, in European and American societies, families with daughters of marriageable age (usually 16) routinely held "coming out" balls for them in hopes of introducing them to a roomful of eligible bachelors. If more than one daughter lived in a household, the younger teenage daughters had to wait until the eldest was given a chance to find a mate. It was considered unfair—as well as imprudent—to flaunt the beauty and attributes of the younger daughters while the eldest was still unmatched.

Rethinking Singleness

In her article "Rethinking the Gift of Singleness," author Debbie Maken writes,

> Even as late as the 1950s, the bachelor was considered a freak for he had avoided the mantle of adulthood in taking on the responsibilities of a wife and family. He was considered "eccentric," a "late bloomer," a man who never really could prove he was a man. An unwed woman was pitied in terms such as "old maid," for she

had been the victim of poor opportunities in the unre-
lenting passage of time. And a few women were rightly
considered "spinsters," for their actions had frustrated
any potential suitors.

Now, compare those beliefs to what singles are told
today. "God is your husband." "Bloom where you are
planted." "There are plenty of ministries you can help
with during this time." "Be content." "Make the desire of
your heart Jesus, not marriage." The desire for marriage
has been placed on a collision course with the desire for
God, the One Who made marriage in the first place.
With this kind of pitting, singles are often reduced to
extolling singleness, much like a witch having the grace
to drown to prove innocence.[2]

Why are Christians today so apt to validate a lifestyle that in the
past would have been considered wayward and abnormal? Borrowing
a phrase from C.S. Lewis, Maken suggests, "Our own 'chronological
snobbery' may make us believe that somehow we know more today
than those who preceded us. However, our contemporary belief that
Scripture validates singleness en masse is a modern invention that has
sprouted only in this generation."[3]

Rather than come to terms with what amounts to a near-crisis in
the church—a bloated demographic of single men and women—the
church has instead "produced a language of holy doublespeak where
adult singleness is thought of as acceptable, even biblical," writes Maken.
"Instead of placing this modern phenomenon of protracted singleness
under [the lens of] Scripture for scrutiny, we have done the exact opposite—we have made Scripture the handmaiden to the phenomenon."[4]

Why Christian Women Are Different

Single Christian women differ from their non-Christian counterparts in one key area: their desire to wait for marriage rather than live

with a man out of wedlock. And for that reason alone, our culture has helped create this generation of lost girls. While everyone else is either married or swept along in the current of cohabitation, these women get left further and further behind *because* of the line they draw in the sand. For a woman not bound by the Mosaic moral code, it's easy to fall into the pattern of the culture—having casual sex to make a relationship "fulfilling"; easing a man toward marriage by living together first (although this approach usually backfires); casual, serial dating that often leaves emotional devastation in its wake.

In her article "Why Not Take Her for a Test Drive?" Jennifer Roback Morse compares couples undergoing a "trial period" of living together to taking a car for a test drive. The analogy breaks down, she admits, when you consider that the car doesn't have hurt feelings after you take it back to the car lot and decide not to buy it. Yet this is precisely the mind-set men and women (unwittingly?) buy into when they live together to see how compatible they are. Writes Morse, "I am going to drive you around the block a few times, withholding judgment and commitment until I have satisfied myself about you. Pay no attention to my indecision, or my periodic evaluations of your performance. Try to act as if we were married, so I can get a clear picture of what you're likely to be like as a spouse. You just pretend to be married; I'll just pretend to be shopping."

In the final analysis, "cohabiting couples have one foot out the door, throughout the relationship," Morse asserts. "They rehearse not trusting."[5] As if the potential for a chronically wounded heart isn't enough, statistics show that even more negative fallout results from living together outside of marriage.

According to Morse,

- Cohabitors are more likely to be depressed than married couples.

- The presence of children exacerbates depression among cohabitors, but not among married couples.

- Cohabiting couples perceive their relationships as less stable.

- Cohabiting couples report poorer relationship quality than married couples.

- Cohabiting women are more likely to have "secondary sex partners" than are married women.

- Cohabiting couples have higher rates of assault, and the violence is more severe, than among dating or married couples.

- Cohabitors tend to be more socially isolated.

- Married couples whose marriages are preceded by cohabitation are more likely to get divorced and to report lower quality marriages.[6]

Cohabitation is one boundary the majority of Christian singles don't cross over, although some do. What is much more common is to remain single for *years*—much longer than earlier generations did—while keeping an eye open for "the one" who might tempt you into marriage. But is this new pattern of dating and mating *normal?* It's a legitimate question. The prevalence of a trend creates the false assumption in our minds that the practice is indeed normal. In reality, it might be the furthest thing from what God intended.

4

SINGLENESS: A HISTORICAL PERSPECTIVE

Spanning history as a whole, singleness has been the anomaly, not the norm. Debbie Maken writes that indeed "past generations of Christians saw singles under a divine obligation," or duty, to get hitched. The "marriage mandate" was woven so intricately into the fabric of Christian society—and, truly, society as a whole—that few questioned it. Maken points out that the institution of marriage itself came with a trifold list of purposes:

- for society (companionship)
- for love (physical affection), and
- for the production of the next generation of the church (children)[1]

Individuals grew up not only with a "duty" to marry, but to do so within a prescribed time frame—in other words, while they were still young. Writes Makin,

> With 1 Corinthians 7 intact in their Bibles, Christians

used to believe that extended singleness had no biblical warrant. The Westminster Confession, for example, lists the "undue delay of marriage" as sin (Q. 139). Even Scripture five times hearkens to the phrase "wife/bridegroom of your youth," not your middle ages, *youth* being the only season that allows one to enjoy the full bundle of rights and privileges of marriage, and to accomplish its generational purposes.

The laws and practices of these former cultures likewise conveyed to all what was normative and what behavior was expected. Throughout the ages, for example, women enjoyed an infrastructure (their family or clan) to see them into the safe harbor of marriage. From arranged marriages to courtship/calling, all conspired to protect and guide women from squandering their best, most fertile years in futility.[2]

In these earlier times and cultures, the "guardians" of the bride screened all would-be suitors based on their worthiness—a suitable career to support his bride after the marriage, right standing in the community, proven character, good breeding, and so forth. "Men were kept on a tight leash in these earlier systems," writes Maken. "Today, we are stuck in a system that is the exact opposite—the balance of power has shifted to some random young man who, though he has virtually unfettered access to the woman, has no binding to her to initiate and bring about a marriage."[3]

Matchmaker, Make Me a Match

Postmodern America has its own forms of matchmaking, to be sure, from singles bars to Internet dating sites to church singles groups to old-fashioned blind dates arranged by friends. We've even seen the revival of the overly romantic idea of mail-order brides (though the reality that follows may not be quite so romantic). But in the last few decades, as American culture and sexual mores have grown more lax, and millions of people have abandoned marriage for living together—or have married and then gotten divorced multiple times—an unexpected new trend has emerged among Christians. Many young women now put off marriage, wanting to pursue exciting careers first, secure in the knowledge that when they're ready to settle down, there will be plenty of available men still swarming around for the choosing.

Meanwhile, rather than seek out mates during their 20s, many Christian males seem to take a cue from the culture and put off marriage for 10, 15, even 20 years or more. Who can blame them, you may say. No one stays married anymore. But, inevitably, when most of these still virile men tire of the dating game and their 40th birthday is approaching, they do some serious thinking and decide it's time to find a wife—and the younger the better. Sure, they may know several attractive women close to their age, but 25 is better than 35, right? This example may seem overly cynical, but it's played out in reality all the time.

Another version of the same trend: A man and woman marry young and perhaps even have children. Years later, divorced and lonely, both start looking for new spouses. The available men on the market that are in the woman's age range either don't want a ready-made family or don't want to start a second family, so again they shop in the lower ages, hoping for a bride who is young and fresh—maybe even virginal. Unless the woman wants to date and/or marry a man much older, she finds her pool of marriageable men (even those who are remarrying) has shrunk drastically.

Friendly Gathering Versus Meat Market

The Christian singles groups of postmodern America got their start in the Jesus Movement era of the 1970s, but the heyday of this new-fangled ministry group was the decade from the mid-80s through the mid-90s. During that decade, "singles ministry" became the buzzword of every large church, and even quite a few small ones. "A lot of cities did a singles metro where two or three thousand singles would gather in one place every week," remembers Brad Goad, singles pastor at the 45,000-member Second Baptist Church of Houston (main campus). "That kind of faded as the Internet grew." He recalls singles retreats he helped facilitate in the early 1990s at large retreat centers, where the attendance would average two thousand. "By the end of the decade it was down to a few hundred, and then last year [2006], it was just one hundred singles."

What caused the change? More churches started doing things locally, and people didn't have to drive as far, says Goad. "It came to a place where the healthy singles who were busy and had careers were fine going to New York City for a weekend with a couple of friends rather than going away to be with two thousand strangers."

While Christian singles groups are the most likely place to turn if you are (a) single and (b) Christian, the groups themselves can often be a source of constant frustration. The shrinking pool of available men is a story you'll hear again and again. You may also notice a peculiar mind-set not present in other meet-up groups: the group will most likely be divided into two subgroups—those who want the focus to be "friends only" and those who hope to encourage men and women to couple off.

The concern, of course, is that what starts out as a wholesome gathering of singles may soon deteriorate into a Christian "meat market." Brad Goad ministers to six hundred singles ages 35 and older (never-married singles, divorced and widowed singles, and single parents) every week. If you include the church's singles of all ages, the number is closer to one thousand. When I asked Goad if he tries to get men and women together, he answered bluntly,

> No; in fact I kind of work against it. We do a lot of social things—dances, etc.—so men and women have plenty of chances to meet on their own. But in our Bible-study

classes, it's definitely not a meat-market kind of thing. Where we have problems are with a lot of the men in their late 30s and early 40s, especially if they want to start a family. They're looking at younger, perhaps more attractive women than someone in their early 40s. Plus, a woman in her mid-40s may not want to have a child. We try to do it as diplomatically as possible, but if we see that there are older guys in classes for younger singles, and we see that they're there with ulterior motives, we'll act as a bouncer of sorts and ask them to leave. It seldom happens, but when it does, it's probably better for them and us that they not be there.

A large church in Orlando ran into the same problem when it revamped its singles program, dividing it into younger and older age groups. Several men from the older group, looking for younger women to date, "crashed" the younger group until word filtered back to the leadership.

While Goad and other singles pastors work hard to avoid the meat-market mentality, they work equally hard at creating opportunities for friendships between men and women. Second Baptist hosts an annual trip to Disney World for several hundred single parents and their kids. Evidently these types of gatherings—what Goad calls a "safe haven" for singles to meet—foster plenty of romance. "I've married several of them off," he reports happily, "and it's the ones who are active and patient and waited for the right one."

Admittedly, other singles functions don't seem to suffer from the same compunction, such as events staged at Jewish community centers. No one makes a pretense about *not* wanting to meet potential mates. Indeed, a Jewish rabbi invented the concept of "speed dating" in hopes of helping young Jewish men and women find prospective mates. At these events, a group of men and women meet and talk to each person of the opposite sex for about three minutes—the amount of time it takes for most people to know whether they want to see someone again. The downside: these types of functions reduce the search for a mate to commodity shopping, and they can leave honest, love-seeking participants feeling jaded and cynical. Just another example of the high cost of living in our "post-courtship" culture, writes Jillian Straus in *Unhooked Generation.*

Christian singles, however, are often encouraged to befriend members of the opposite sex but not pursue romance, as Brad Goad said. This may seem all well and good until *years* go by, and everybody is still "just friends." At that point I have to wonder, What happened to marriage? When do the endless round of singles functions bear fruit for the majority of Christian singles? In our quest to "kiss dating goodbye," as author Joshua Harris did, have we unwittingly kissed marriage goodbye too?

Though he's often blamed for sanctioning perpetual singleness, the apostle Paul never set marriage and singleness on an equal plane, states author Debbie Maken. "Paul acknowledged celibacy (i.e., the supernatural removal of sexual desire) as a God-given gift. He acknowledged that the celibate could be single, but that the single could not necessarily be celibate and therefore [he] prescribed marriage."[4]

To Marry or to Burn?

In his first letter to the church at Corinth, the apostle Paul wrote,

> But I say to the unmarried and to the widows: It is good for them if they remain even as I am; but if they cannot exercise self-control, let them marry. For it is better to marry than to burn with passion. Now to the married I command, yet not I but the Lord: A wife is not to depart from her husband (1 Corinthians 7:8-10).

This controversial statement regarding singles contains two elements that trip people up.

On the one hand, Paul admonishes unmarried people to remain "even as I am"; that is, single. Then on the heels of this pronouncement, he says, "But if they cannot exercise self-control, let them marry." These are two very distinct states of being, yet modern Christian singles tend to lump the supernatural gift of celibacy and ordinary singleness into a confused whole. As the years go by, we berate ourselves for struggling with our own God-given sexuality, and then as a society (or at least as a Christian subculture), we make it difficult to pair off in marriage.

I believe Paul is really saying, "If you don't have this supernatural gift of celibate singleness God has granted me, then it's better for you to marry than to struggle with sexual temptations." You don't have to look far to realize that most people aren't "blessed" with supernatural celibacy—far from it. From Catholic priests denied access to marriage (some of whom turn to altar boys for sexual pleasure) to ordinary men and women caught in a time warp of perpetual singleness, hormones rage the way God intended them to. We weren't meant to live lives of protracted singleness.

"God is often painted as capriciously willing singleness for some and not for others," writes Debbie Maken. "Consequently and sadly, many Christian singles resign themselves to this less-than-ideal state. A more thoughtful and critical examination reveals that today's singleness is not some sort of divinely ordained, interminable state for a quarter of the population, but the result of a string of systematic impediments to marriage."[5]

So where have we gone wrong? Maken spells out the impediments:

- a male-friendly mating structure that is not geared toward marriage, but toward low-commitment, short-term, shallow cyclical relationships
- a low view of marriage, with the process to achieve it reflecting its value: the casual nature of dating

ultimately reflects the casual nature with which we treat our marriages

- lack of male leadership in the home, with parents bringing up boys to remain boys

- a protracted education system that doesn't really educate

- the removal of shame for indulging in the Indian Summer of one's adolescence or for being a perennial bachelor

- a privatized version of the meaning of marriage

- a diminished expectation of marriage from the divorce culture, and

- a redefinition or a defining downward of healthy biblical adulthood[6]

As she delivers her final argument in this treatise on singleness, Maken summarizes with this shocking statement:

> In the church, instead of acknowledging that singles are operating in the *most dysfunctional mating scheme known to world history,* we simply presume on the Lord and his sovereignty to override our collective recklessness. Instead of recognizing that many single women are victims because of the deficits in the present construct, we dismiss their unwanted status as simply "God's will."

> Today's singleness is not celibacy-induced kingdom work unaccommodating to family life. No, it's the result of choices and mistakes by both the individual and society. Today's singleness is either a lifestyle option or purely circumstantial; therefore, it is largely unbiblical" (emphasis added).[7]

Sometimes the "choices and mistakes" we and society make get so entrenched in our thinking that we blindly follow the prescribed patterns, whether we intend to or not. One such pattern—Christian men not asking women out—is particularly unsettling. That's where we'll go next in our discussion.

WHY CHRISTIAN MEN AREN'T DATING

The older I get as a single-again Christian woman, the more I notice a disturbing trend that I can't quite account for: Christian men, by and large, don't pursue women and ask them out on dates. Now, the sheer fact that there are married Christian couples out there seems to make hash of my observation—obviously, at some point these husbands pursued the women who eventually became their wives. But start asking around among small groups of single Christian women and you'll see what I mean. Their frustration with the dating scene—or lack thereof—in Christian circles is so common, you begin to hear a refrain.

"What's up with Christian guys?" my friend Whitney lamented. "I went to the Keys with three girlfriends, and guys hit on us all the time [they declined]. Yet here at home, in our Christian singles groups, we can't even get a guy to acknowledge us, let alone ask for a date."

Janet told me that a guy in her Bible study has been paying a lot of attention to her lately, but every time he calls, he asks if she wants to "grab a bite to eat"—with him *and* his roommate.

Crystal has a different complaint. She met a wonderful Christian man on the tennis court and got to know him gradually over several months, until their casual friendship deepened into what she thought was something more. When he invited her over for dinner, she was sure he was taking their relationship to the next level. After the second such dinner, the two of them watched a movie together on the sofa, enjoying an evening of laughter and innocent companionship. Then the unexpected happened. The guy "dropped off the face of the earth," Crystal said. Two weeks passed with no word from him, no friendly phone call—nada. Finally, both puzzled and frustrated, she called him and asked how things were. He stammered that they needed to be just friends and all but slammed a door in her face.

You might be tempted to chalk it up to the common male malady of commitment phobia, but the sheer volume of such stories out there makes me wonder.

Undoubtedly, many Christian singles were impacted by Joshua Harris's best-selling book *I Kissed Dating Goodbye,* in which he recommends interacting with the opposite sex in groups until you find "the one" and are ready for courtship—intentional dating with an eye toward marriage. But it seems unlikely that this mind-set accounts for the overwhelming lack of dating among Christians because so many Christian singles don't espouse Harris's viewpoint. Again, casual conversations (in this case, with men) shed light on the subject. Wanting to get to the core of the issue, I asked a few guys in my own singles Bible study what was up.

"I can tell you what it is," said one male friend emphatically. "They're scared. Christian guys are scared to get involved with girls because they hear in church about the dangers of getting too close to someone [physically]."

"If a girl is mature, and I'm interested in her, then maybe I'll ask her out [on a casual date], but otherwise it can be a bad idea," said one guy friend who just turned 42 and has never been married.

Not sure what his vague response meant, I pressed for an explanation. He'd been burned more than once, it seems, by women who mistook a "casual date" to mean he was seriously considering them as wife candidates. Backpedaling his way out of those sticky situations wasn't worth the trouble anymore.

"Anytime I sit in church with a new girl, everyone swoops down on me later and wants to know if it's serious and whether she's the one," lamented yet another male friend, who rolled his eyes as he told his story. Eventually the "big news" traveled around the whole church.

Then there was Bryan, a 45-year-old man who's been married only three years but remembers well the trepidation he and his single Christian brothers faced in the church. "They're scared," he said. "So many guys are petrified of the idea of commitment, and of course there's the whole issue of staying morally pure. For a lot of guys, it's easier to just avoid the whole thing."

But he did finally get married, I reminded him. Then I asked how he got to know his wife. Did they date?

"We didn't date in the traditional sense of the word," Bryan said. "We were around each other in groups all the time, and one day I just sort of noticed her in a new way. We were friends for a long time before I knew I wanted her to be my wife."

I can hear Joshua Harris cheering somewhere.

Our frustrations aside, we Christian women have to acknowledge that sometimes we're part of the problem, whether we're smothering a guy, pressuring him to act, dismissing potential candidates worthy of a second look, or simply not acting "datable"; that is, being the kind of godly women that godly men are looking for.

Desperately Seeking a Man

I'm about to say something that will make feminists livid and the rest of my female sisterhood, well, perhaps embarrassed: If we're honest, most of us are desperate for a man—and it shows.

One day as I was flipping through a women's fashion magazine, an article caught my eye. The headline boldly proclaimed, "Get a Life Without a Man!" and it drew me in. Lots of rah-rah verbiage followed, assuring women they didn't have to wait for a man for their lives to be complete. The article outlined the many ways a woman's life can be enriched minus the presence of Mr. Right—or even Mr. Almost Right, I read between the lines.

All good stuff, but then I flipped a few pages ahead and found a feature that shouted, "How to Tell If He Loves You: The Little Signs That Give Him Away." Another article listed ways women could better entice men, and yet another divulged secrets for spicing up women's love lives. As an aside, I found myself counting the number of times the magazine used valuable page real estate to talk about how to please men, allure men, understand men, cook for men, get back at men, befriend men, and so on. The irony clanged like a gong.

On my next convenience-store run, I eyed the covers of two prominent men's magazines while waiting to pay at the counter. You can probably guess what I found there: cover lines about beating the competition (other males), must-have vehicles, the latest electronic-gadgets wish list, how to succeed at work, and, oh yes, ways to make a woman swoon. Later at home I surfed Web sites like FHM *(For Him Magazine)* and GQ *(Gentlemen's Quarterly)*. Again, none of the pleading, desperate, *hungry* verbiage that I found in the women's magazine. To be fair, women's magazines contain plenty of information about beauty, makeup, fashion, home décor, health, and organizing your life, but the balance of need-the-opposite-sex articles tips the scale far lower on the female side. Despite our bold independence and busy lives, it seems we women are still desperate to catch a man after all.

A Good Man Is Hard to Find

In the Christian singles "Why can't I find a mate?" milieu, it's both easy and convenient to lay the blame on men, but that would tell only part of the story. In the interest of fairness, however, the male half of the story warrants attention. A 2002 National Marriage Project study found that modern men have a hard time committing because of the following ten reasons:

1. They can get sex without marriage more easily than in times past.

2. They can enjoy the benefits of having a wife by cohabiting rather than marrying.

3. They want to avoid divorce and its financial risks.

4. They want to wait until they are older to have children.

5. They fear that marriage will require too many changes and compromises.

6. They are waiting for the perfect soul mate and she hasn't yet appeared.

7. They face few social pressures to marry.

8. They are reluctant to marry a woman who already has children.

9. They want to own a house before they get a wife.

10. They want to enjoy single life as long as they can.[1]

It wasn't always this way. Once upon a time men pursued women with intentions to marry because otherwise they wouldn't have the sexual benefits of marriage. And so, in a very real sense, women were the gatekeepers of intimacy, regulating when men had access to the delights of physical pleasure by withholding it until they (the women) were safely ensconced in a marriage covenant. This relational process, which was considered normal and morally right for thousands of years, was reinforced by cultural standards. Society expected young men to grow up much earlier than they do today, and part of that growing up naturally meant taking a wife.

In Search of Something Better

Our culture's loss of restraint, our lack of inhibitions, our anything-goes attitude—all have given us the illusion of freedom, but we've paid a heavy price in the trade. Instead of love, we have lust. Instead of commitment, we have trial-run relationships. Instead of marriage, we have cohabitation. Those who still do believe in marriage—Christian singles included—often find themselves so jaded by the divorce statistics, or the real-life experiences of people they know, that they put off marriage beyond the most reasonable age for getting a mate (mid-20s to early 30s) out of fear or its strange cousin: holding out for the elusive "something better" that may be just around the corner, or what social-theory professor Barry Schwartz calls "the paradox of choice" in his book by the same name.

He writes,

> When people have no choice, life is almost unbearable. As the number of available choices increases…the autonomy, control, and liberation this variety brings are powerful and positive. But as the number of choices keeps growing, negative aspects of having a multitude of options begin to appear. As the number of choices grows further, the negatives escalate until we become overloaded. At this point, choice no longer liberates, but debilitates. It might even be said to tyrannize.[2]

Boundless writer Thomas Jeffries discussed the very real predicament of too many choices when it comes to life-altering decisions:

> What about when it's time to settle on your first investment, a new car or the person you'll commit to for life? How are you supposed to make such an important selection when a "better" choice could be right around the corner? If you're the type of person who has trouble deciding on a wireless plan, then you're in for a rough ride ahead.[3]

In discussing the big question, or "the" decision, Jeffries next turns to Jillian Straus, author of *Unhooked Generation: The Truth About*

Why We're Still Single, who writes that our consumer-oriented society has created "a sense that countless options exist, options that make it difficult to commit to one person." Straus explains:

> No longer hoping to meet someone by chance at church or a dinner party, the creation of an online community suggests that our true soul mate might be just one more click away. These communities of singles in urban areas, artificially created by the Internet, have resulted in a vast dating marketplace. In a marketplace with so many choices, the notion of finding your soul mate can seem daunting at best. Yet the promise always exists that if one relationship doesn't work out or gets old, you can log on for something better. With a glut of choices, it is easy to see why so many men and women remain single, despite their search for their "one and only." [4]

As one male survey respondent wrote, "We have a toy store in front of us as we look for Mr. or Miss Right, so we pass for something better."

Curiously, among those singles who don't fear marriage or hold out for perfection, they find themselves caught in the grip of a nameless societal malaise that renders marriage a thing to be put off indefinitely.

One female survey respondent in her late 40s sees this malaise as the product of a vast cultural experiment that went awry, an experiment that got its start with the feminist movement of the 60s and 70s. She writes,

> I think men have undergone a personality crisis en masse, beginning with the wave of feminism in the 1970s. I think that as women have become stronger, men have become weaker, as if they don't know what to do except the opposite. I think this can also be seen in the very modern trend of alpha working wives and

stay-at-home dads...As the mother of a son, I can tell you that males have a natural tendency to be lazy if there is a strong woman around who will pick up the slack for them. And this, my friends, is the crux of the matter, in my opinion. It's a massive societal change, not unlike other massive societal changes in history: the baby boom, the revolutionary era, the era of dictatorships, and so on. We're caught up in a historical tidal wave in changing human relations, but we can't really see it yet because not enough time has gone by to give us the proper perspective. This huge societal trend is partly why I've stopped struggling in the rip current anymore, instead just floating on it, letting it wildly carry me away from the populated beach wherever it wants to—down the shoreline to a more deserted stretch of beach, most likely (in other words, single forever)!

Delayed Marriage Fallout

In *Unhooked Generation,* Jillian Straus labels "the fallout from the marriage delay" as Evil Influence number seven, adding that this massive social experiment has become "both a cause and an effect of a noncommitment culture. Falling in love for the first time is easy: expectations are few, cynicism is minimal," writes Straus. "Once you've done it more than once, though, skepticism can set in and baggage accumulates."[5]

For the first time in U.S. history, both men and women are choosing to marry later in life than any preceding generation did. The average marrying age today is 27 for men and 25 for women. While the delay gives people time to grow up, Straus contends, it also starts the process toward *extended* delay. And soon delay becomes a habit. Since few single men and women stay relationship-free in their 20s (outside of marriage), that means they will absorb more heartbreak from failed romances than their parents did at the same age.

Curiously, the marriage delay also raises the stakes of a relationship, Straus asserts. "Obviously, women facing the pressure of their biological clocks are at a disadvantage in a culture in which potential male partners face fewer physical pressures to commit." And unfortunately, as a woman ages, she may become less desirable because of both her decrease in fertility and the scrutiny of a youth-obsessed culture. She may face aging out of the dating market."[6]

One never-married woman in her early 30s reflected on another inadvertent side-effect of delaying marriage: waiting for perfection.

> We as a church are so often taught in this day and age that things have to be "perfectly" in order, that emotionally we have to be just right, that financially we have to be perfect, that if we don't have the perfect relationship with God, we can't go out and have a nice time, that it isn't about just dating to check out someone, but the pressure is there to decide within a first or second date whether that person is the "one."

To her credit, she adds, "I'd be the first to admit that I'm often the one who puts this pressure on a relationship."

One can almost hear a wistful sigh at the end of Straus' summation, as if to say, "Yes, society has changed, but we (women) are the losers." Reading between the lines—and sometimes directly in the text—of dozens of survey responses from women, I came away with the feeling that they long for what their grandmothers had. As Wendy Shalit, author of the groundbreaking book *A Return to Modesty: Discovering the Lost Virtue,* observes, "We're not flocking to Jane Austen movies because we want the facts, but because we're sick of having the facts shoved in our faces all the time."[7] Or, as one young woman told me, "It's like the T-shirt that says 'I Heart Mr. Darcy.' "

Where is the beauty and mystery and thrilling inhibition that God intended to mark the relationship between men and women? We long for it, but we're also partly to blame for its demise. Like Esau, we traded our birthright for a mess of pottage.

It's unrealistic to expect our culture to transform into a throwback of an earlier generation, but taking stock of what those generations did right might help us turn the tide in the proper direction and recapture some of what we've lost. As it turns out, one could even surmise that women are more to blame for the current marriage crisis than men could ever be. Men are simply taking their cues from us.

6

THE ALLURE
OF MODESTY

In *A Return to Modesty,* Wendy Shalit makes a potent case for how a loss of modesty on the part of *women* brought us to our present crisis:

> In essence, a culture that respects a specifically female type of modesty is one that regulates and informs the relations between the sexes in a nuanced...way. Women who dress and act "modestly" conduct themselves in ways that shroud their sexuality in mystery. They live in a way that makes womanliness more a transcendent, implicit quality than a crude, explicit quality. When Peter urged Christian wives to reject the current fashions of the world around them, he didn't tell them to be ugly. Instead he enjoined them to take on a more eternal kind of beauty...More recently, the *Sunday Gazette Mail* reports that "women appear to be relying on the power within rather than powerful dressing without." It is respect for this "power within" that once made it

impossible for men to view women merely as sexual objects. Rather, women became something deeper, more elemental: possessors of a deep and wondrous secret that is revealed only to the one who proves himself deserving of her.[1]

Danielle Crittenden touches on this same sentiment in her best-selling book *What Our Mothers Didn't Tell Us: Why Happiness Eludes the Modern Woman,* explaining why what we women traded away—our collective sense of propriety for the freedom to be independent and sexually uninhibited—came at such a high price:

> Indeed, in all the promises made to us about our ability to achieve freedom and independence as women, the promise of sexual emancipation may have been the most illusory. These days, certainly, it is the one most brutally learned…The unfair, ugly fact about the mating dance is that so much of female sexual power depends upon withholding oneself. If anything, that is even truer in an age when all the other girls are available, too.[2]

Harking back to more genteel eras, Wendy Shalit goes on to write about the extreme deference men showed toward women, and the cultivation of manners, reinforced by society, that turned men into gentlemen. Women acted like ladies, like they deserved to be treated as special, and so they were.

One male survey respondent weighed in on this topic and what could be called a pining away for old-fashioned girls: "It's getting increasingly harder to tell the difference between Christians and non-Christians. I find many women who say they're Christians but do things like sleep around, have live-in boyfriends, drink to get drunk, smoke, and curse…Where are these attractive, eligible single women you speak of?"

Women Men Marry

Men are drawn to female modesty despite our culture's bold declaration to the contrary. Most women can probably think of a time when their own modest behavior elicited a sense of awe from men in our otherwise leering, lewd society. One such encounter stands out vividly in my mind. Raised to be a lady, I had nonetheless lived the party lifestyle during my teenage-rebellion years and experienced the uglier side of male behavior. So imagine my surprise one day years later, after becoming a Christian, when I found myself having to pass by a group of construction workers at my job site and met with…quiet respect. Their response floored me.

I remember distinctly that I was wearing a dress that day at work, modestly cut but attractive. As I approached the area and spotted the group of men, a feeling of dread washed over me, but I whispered a prayer for protection, kept my head up, my eyes down, and passed by in total silence. It was as if someone cast a spell over the men, and the effect was palpable. Their noisy male jostling ceased, and as I walked by, not one lewd remark or wolf whistle followed me. Maybe you could chalk it up to the power of prayer that day, and I like to think God did play a part, but I can't help but think the transformation in *me* was partly responsible for the men's reaction. I now regarded myself as a lady, someone of value and worth in God's eyes, and I believe I emanated that to the world.

A story I heard years ago on this subject still lingers in my memory. The pastor of the church I attended told how he and his wife had a stopover in Las Vegas on a trip out west. Needing to stay overnight, they booked a room in one of the large hotels that had a casino on the first floor. My pastor described the scene: the crowded casino, a roomful of drinking men and women showing too much of their bodies. Passing through the crowd to the registration desk, he let his wife go ahead of him and marveled at what happened. He watched as, in this room filled with overexposed women oozing sensuality, the men parted like the Red Sea to allow his beautiful and modestly dressed wife pass to the registration desk, staring quietly after her the whole way. Suddenly, in that moment, the other women figuratively disappeared from view.

This lovely woman died several years later, but I still remember her vividly. She was beautiful, yes, but it was more than that. She carried herself like a queen in the best sense of the word. Regal yet undemanding. Beautiful yet chaste. Feminine and alluring but not in the least bit outwardly sensual.

Yes, men are aroused by sultry women who flaunt their sensuality and their bodies as a form of power. They may be helplessly turned on by the many alluring sexual images our culture throws out as bait. But the women they marry are usually the ones whose sensuality is much more hidden from view—there for the right man, but not on display for all the world to see.

Beauty and Chastity—a Potent Combination

Have we as a culture, as women, lost something more potent than we realized while we still had it? Wendy Shalit believes so, and her argument—not to mention the record of recent history—offers convincing evidence. In a chapter titled "Modesty and the Erotic," she writes,

> Seemingly every year, another study announces that married women are more orgasmic than single women. At first I wonder, Do I really need to know this detail? But then I read on and I am transfixed. Married women generally feel safer, which our scientists report is a precondition for being able to relax...After surveying 100,000 women, *Redbook* magazine found that the most strongly religious women were "more responsive sexually" than all other women. Everyone, including the scientists themselves, is always surprised when these studies are released because we have been taught that the

married are oppressed, the religious are boring squares, and the swinging singles are the ones having all the fun. But maybe that's only because we misunderstand sexual modesty. [If we] set beside these mysterious studies Balzac's quip that "the most virtuous women have in them something which is never chaste"...we have an even thornier problem. If a return to modesty can save a generation of women from the ravages of a culture that affords us precious little respect or protection, then how can it also be that modesty seems, at times, more exciting?"[3]

Shalit goes on to describe the first time she came across John Kasson's photographic essay "Amusing the Million: Coney Island at the Turn of the Century." Amazed and charmed by the quaint, sepia-tone pictures and "how civilized everyone looked," Shalit was surprised to learn that these young men and women smiling shyly at the camera were in fact being *bad.* "It turns out that unchaperoned young men and women used to flock to Coney Island in order to perch on amusement rides which contrived to *seat them close together,* and often they would even *get engaged to be married there.* What world was this, where getting engaged could sound like a dirty thing, and where people could misbehave in jackets, ties, hats, dresses, and parasols?" Shalit summarizes this portion of her chapter with this statement: "Certainly sexual modesty may damp down superficial allure, the kind of allure that inspires a one-night stand. But the kind of allure that lasts—that is what modesty protects and inspires."[4]

Earlier in the book, Shalit describes her introduction to what she calls "modestyniks," her term for Jewish men and women practicing the laws of *tzniut,* or sexual modesty before marriage. She sees a "curious picture" of a modern, young Jewish woman with her betrothed. Though grinning widely, the engaged couple are standing very close together but don't have their arms around each other. Indeed, Shalit detects a thin blue line of sky between the two of them. Close, but not touching. She writes, "How strange, I thought: If they didn't really like each other, then why in the world did they get married?"

The second picture of the same couple shows them at their wedding. This time they're looking not at the camera but at each other. "Specifically," Shalit writes, "he was gazing down at her and she up at him. Now they were embracing each other very tightly. Upon seeing this particular picture, I felt tears float up to my eyes. I hoped the next photo would arrive soon enough to distract me, but unfortunately it didn't quite, and I was left blubbering for an excruciating eight seconds."[5]

A third photo showed the now-married couple on the beach. The young bride held a baby boy in her arms and wore a black straw hat on her head—the married woman's head covering required by Orthodox Jewish tradition.

"That's how I learned that there are different stages in the life cycle of a modestynik," Shalit concludes. "No Touching, Touching, then Hat. Okay, I figured, I could remember that...All around me I started to hear, and read, about young women who were observing Jewish modesty law, not touching their boyfriends and suddenly sporting hats. All with the same blue line of sky between them and their fiancés. All with the same modestynik twinkle at the end. It was like an epidemic."[6]

Others would whisper about these strange throwbacks to an earlier time, Shalit observes. Modern young men and women (in New York City, of all places) out of step with their generation and the sexual liberations their parents had won for them. Or they would blame the girls' "sexual repression" on what must have been a bad experience in their past, or perhaps even an abusive father. But as Shalit encountered more and more modestyniks and observed their "normalness," she got suspicious. "If all modestyniks were really abuseniks, I asked myself, then why were they so twinkly? Why did they seem so contented? Why were their wedding pictures so viscerally and mysteriously moving?"[7]

Shalit speaks for more single women—and certainly single Christian women—than she may realize. In the conversations I had with women, as well as the survey responses that poured in, an unmistakable sadness and frustration surfaced regarding the *very times we live in,* as if these women wanted to say, *Why couldn't I have been born a hundred years ago, when things were sweeter and simpler between men and women?*

Ultimately, it appears that single Christian women who long for marriage but seem unable to find it are caught in the riptide of a culture gone awry. As we'll see in the next chapter, not only do the rules change for older singles looking to marry, but so do the players themselves. For some, it feels like a whole new ball game.

WHO MOVED MY ALTar?

In her best-selling book *Find a Husband After 35*, Rachel Greenwald outlines six major differences that set older single women apart—specifically ages 35 and up—from their 20-something sisters. Because our discussion deals with the phenomenon of so many single women in the church, Greenwald's input is invaluable. And although she's talking about single women in general, her points apply equally well for the subset of Christian singles. Either way, with the passage of years, the challenges of dating grow. According to Greenwald, six major differences come into play for single women in their 30s and beyond:

1. *Urgency.* By the time a woman hits her (mid-) 30s, a sense of urgency underlines her life. Suddenly her biological clock starts ticking, and every promising date leaves her thinking, *Could he be the one?* Well-meaning friends and family are asking, "Why aren't you married yet?"

2. *Fewer single men.* "It's a math equation that's hard to grasp," writes Greenwald. "There should be

roughly an equal number of single men after 35 as there are women, right? Wrong…" One attributable factor: many men marry younger women.

3. *Changed bodies.* As time progresses onward, our bodies progress downward—literally. By the mid-30s, Greenwald asserts, "you are more likely to have problem body areas."

4. *Baggage.* We all accumulate more "baggage" as we age, whether it be kids, ex-spouses, ex-boyfriends or girlfriends, out-of-control debt, or emotional hang-ups. The pool of men we look to as potential mates have more baggage by now too.

5. *Habits.* Over time we tend to get set in our ways. It really is harder to teach an old dog new tricks (okay, an older dog!).

6. *Insular lifestyle.* By your mid-30s, your life is more insular. "You aren't on a college campus where thousands of single men hang around…Your job may be in a smaller office environment as you've risen higher in your position, or in a smaller city where it seems harder to meet eligible men," writes Green-wald. "Most of your friends are married with kids, and socializing means being a third wheel. You're probably in a personal rut, doing the same things over and over with the same circle of people."[1]

Typical of human nature, the women who took my survey largely blamed men for their still-single status, and the men likewise blamed women. However, our experiences in other fields of endeavor show that this can't always be true, and in fact, some might say the exact opposite comes closer to reality: We're largely responsible for the way our lives turn out. While times do change and sweeping cultural shifts may happen to otherwise innocent people (e.g., in the early 1940s, young men went off to war, leaving few at home to marry eligible women), we're seldom truly helpless in their wake.

A woman doesn't become a lost girl overnight. It's usually a slow progression—and a series of lifestyle choices. In his book *Why Men Marry Some Women and Not Others,* market researcher and corporate consultant John Molloy identifies six factors that set apart women who eventually marry from those who don't:

1. Women who marry insist on marriage. They settle for nothing else.

2. Women who married were far less likely to have wasted their time in dead-end relationships.

3. Women who married loved themselves more than they loved any man.

4. Women who are committed to the idea of marriage are much more likely to marry than those who are not.

5. Women who are slender have an easier time meeting men and better odds of getting married.

6. Time is the single woman's enemy. Use time wisely in your search for a man who wants to marry.[2]

After poring over numerous love/romance books and articles, I've come to the realization that almost every "expert" agrees on one key point: There comes a time in any dating relationship, or exclusive man-woman "friendship," when the man needs to make his intentions known. If he doesn't, he may need a few subtle hints from the woman. She makes a mistake if she allows him to wallow in the comfort zone of no commitment for too long. Several women who responded to my survey called this time when a man declares his intentions "stepping up to the plate," either in the initial act of asking a woman out or in the much more serious act of proposing marriage. When a woman has to "help" a man get to this stage, it's rarely something she wants to do, but it may be the turning point that leads to a successful match. *Boundless* Webzine founding editor Candice Watters calls this "pulling a Ruth," a phrase she learned in college.

"Pulling a Ruth"

As Watters relates, she and her now-husband, Steve, became good friends in college and frequently hung out together. "We weren't dating and the relationship was platonic," she writes. "But I was hopeful." On the drive home from a day-long social event, Steve suddenly announced he had to get back to campus early because he had a date—with another woman. Reeling from shock, Watters nonetheless kept her feelings to herself. The school year passed by in a haze of friendship, but by summer they were spending time together every day, and everyone else thought they were a couple. Steve was no longer dating anyone else, but neither had he declared Candice his girlfriend. "I was at my wits' end," she writes. "Here was the man I wanted to marry and he was oblivious to what a good match we were."

The event that followed changed the course of their lives. Watters recounts:

> Enter Mary Morken. Mary was the wife of one of our professors and with a little digging, we discovered that she had quite a reputation for matching couples—over 30 to date. Back at the beginning of the school year, I had joined several female friends to organize a retreat. Of course it was all part of our plan to get the Morkens in a casual environment where they could tell us—and our male classmates—about their romance.
>
> They agreed...As we gathered around the stone fireplace, Mary told about how she and Hubert Morken had been close friends at Wheaton [College] many years before...

Mary admitted she had been in love with Hubert all along, but never let on. She prayed God would open his eyes and worked at being the best friend to him she could be. Listening to her speak, I couldn't help but notice the similarities between her story and mine. I was desperate for more information, and advice.

After they finished, they took questions. Mary talked about why the times we live in make it so hard for marriages to form. "The culture we live in is anti-marriage," she said. "So many of the customs and unwritten social rules that once helped bring young men and women together, now seem to pull them apart."

A light went off in my head—I hadn't realized what I was up against. Up till then, I thought just praying for a husband was enough.

I didn't waste a minute. "So what can we do about it?!" Mary responded matter-of-factly: "Sometimes you have to 'Pull a Ruth.'"[3]

The biblical story of Ruth centers on a young widow who leaves her homeland after the death of her husband to travel to a foreign country with her widowed mother-in-law, Naomi, who wants to return to the land of her people (the Hebrews). Still young enough to marry, Ruth insists on staying with her mother-in-law. In Bethlehem Ruth goes out to glean from the harvest fields belonging to a rich man named Boaz, who shows her great favor. When Naomi realizes that Ruth is gleaning in the fields of a close relative—a kinsman-redeemer—she advises Ruth to present herself to him as a prospective bride:

> Then Naomi her mother-in-law said to her, "My daughter, shall I not seek security for you, that it may be well with you? Now Boaz, whose young women you were

with, is he not our relative? In fact, he is winnowing barley tonight at the threshing floor. Therefore wash yourself and anoint yourself, put on your best garment and go down to the threshing floor; but do not make yourself known to the man until he has finished eating and drinking. Then it shall be, when he lies down, that you shall notice the place where he lies; and you shall go in, uncover his feet, and lie down; and he will tell you what you should do."

And she said to her, "All that you say to me I will do."

...Now it happened at midnight that the man was startled, and turned himself; and there, a woman was lying at his feet. And he said, "Who are you?" So she answered, "I am Ruth, your maidservant. Take your maidservant under your wing, for you are a close relative" (Ruth 3:1-5,8-9).

The story has a happy ending: Boaz takes Ruth as his wife. But before everything is neatly wrapped up, while there is still uncertainty hanging in the air, Naomi speaks my favorite words in this story: "Sit still, my daughter, until you know how the matter will turn out; for the man will not rest until he has concluded the matter this day" (verse 18).

Once a little healthy pressure is put on a man, he can't "rest" until he settles the matter. The answer may be no, or, as in Watters' case, it may be yes. Either way, closure is brought to the situation—and that's a whole lot better than floundering miserably in uncertainty.

"I was ready to follow [Ruth's] lead," writes Watters. "Now all I needed was the modern-day application."[4] She goes on to tell the end of the story:

On our way to campus the morning before summer break was over, I laid it all on the line. "Steve, I want to get married and I hope it's to you. But if it's not, then we need to stop spending all this time together. Otherwise, no one else will ask me out—they all think we're dating." I said it in one breath, my heart pounding out of my chest. He was listening.

"I need you to call this what it is. I can't just be the buddy who gives you someone to hang out with on the weekends and all the days in between. Are we dating or not?"

I was asking him to lead. I was serious about being willing to walk away from him and he knew it.

We agreed to spend the day apart and get back together that evening to talk…

He picked me up after dinner and we went for a walk at dusk around a small lake on campus. When we finished the circle and sat down on a bench, my hands were trembling. I couldn't guess what he would say. He wasn't giving me any hints.

I remember the intensity in his eyes when he said yes.

God answered my prayers that day. Steve opened his heart and with the advice of the Morkens, he "let love grow" between us…Six months later, Steve got down on one knee in a small garden in Williamsburg, VA, and asked me to be his wife.

Then it was my turn to say yes.[5]

Based on the results of my survey, this desire for men to step up to the plate is the number one frustration single Christian women have with the single Christian men they encounter. So, what if you find yourself in a position of having to "pull a Ruth"? First of all, as a woman myself, I implore the single men reading this book, *Don't make us have to get that drastic!* No woman wants to feel like she's goading a man toward the altar—much less a first date—so take the initiative to ask us out. I guarantee you, women *love* to be pursued; in fact, we long for it.

The Ultimatum

If things are moving along promisingly in your relationship and then get stalled, it may be time to give a guy an ultimatum, declaring that you insist on dating exclusively, entering a traditional courtship phase (with the intention of marrying), or getting engaged outright. Sometimes the only way a man appreciates what he's got is when he knows he stands a real chance of losing it. Author John Molloy states bluntly that if a woman senses a man is wasting her time, she needs to give him a deadline. If he hasn't proposed by that point, she should move on.

If you find yourself in the uncomfortable position of needing to "pull a Ruth," cover the situation in prayer. Saturate it in prayer. Candice Watters did. I skipped over this paragraph in the initial excerpt for brevity's sake, but it bears stating now. During their day of separation to sort out their hearts, Candice writes, "I spent the hours thinking and praying; asking God to embolden Steve and open his heart to love. I knew with all of my being that we would be a good match. But I also knew that palling around wasn't getting me any closer to my goal—and calling—of marriage. So I also prayed for my own strength to follow through if he said no."[6]

Earlier, as the months of friendship stretched on before her, Watters writes,

> Prayer played no small part in our budding romance. Since Steve had not yet made any commitment to me, I couldn't share the secrets of my heart with him—I had to rely on the Lord. My journals from those months of

waiting are filled with prayers for patience and trust and ultimately, God's will. I knew that as much as I wanted Steve, I wanted even more to be in God's will. So I prayed that God's plan included Steve—and if it didn't, that He would change the desires of my heart.[7]

What is that elusive *something* that makes one man spark with one woman? What are we, as single Christian men and women, doing right or wrong in our pursuit of true love? In the next two sections, we'll pull back the veil to reveal what real-world singles *really* think about the opposite sex—and desperately wish they could tell them.

PART 2

WHAT women say...

"we want to be pursued, and men won't step up to the plate!"

(Guys aren't asking us out • Guys today are too passive
• Men need to start being men • Men are afraid of commitment)

*For a woman, it was not enough to be "struck with love," in the
phrase of the day; she must await a lover. While a man might have
the illusion of control, a woman knew that her role in the early
stages of courtship was a reactive one: she might accept, defer, or
decline a suitor's offer. Men might claim it was "ladies to whom all
matrimonial causes are ultimately referred," but an observant young
woman like Eliza Southgate could see that "the inequality of privi-
lege between the sexes is…in no instance…greater than in the liberty
of choosing a partner in marriage; true, we have the liberty of refus-
ing those we don't like, but not of selecting those we do."[1]*

ELLEN K. ROTHMAN,
HANDS AND HEARTS: A HISTORY OF
COURTSHIP IN AMERICA

We should be woo'd and were not made to woo.

WILLIAM SHAKESPEARE,
A MIDSUMMER NIGHT'S DREAM

You don't have to be among single Christian women very long to
hear one common refrain, "We want to be pursued," followed close
on its heels by "Why won't guys ask us out?" As I sifted through the
survey data and started tallying women's responses, this one topic

took up so much space, literally, that it demanded lead position in this section.

In Eliza Southgate's day (see opening quote) women understood that their romantic lot in life was one of waiting to be pursued. Likewise, Helena in Shakespeare's *A Midsummer Night's Dream* learns quickly how frustrating it is to be on the pursuing end of the stick when you're a woman. Today many would argue that women enjoy the right, even the freedom, to pursue men if they choose, without ruffling any societal feathers. A woman can be the first to call a guy she's just met. She can flirt with him via e-mail. She can even ask him out on a date. And all the secular women's magazines will applaud her for her gutsy behavior. Yet almost every woman surveyed for this book expressed views that are polar opposite to this bold stance: They want to be pursued, or "wooed and won," as an earlier generation called it.

I once read a magazine article with the opener, "How did a generation of women grow up wanting to marry Edward Rochester?" The protagonist of Charlotte Brontë's classic *Jane Eyre* is dark, brooding, intelligent, quick-witted, yet cynical. Still, for all his negative qualities (Jane herself describes him as "not handsome"), Rochester manages to captivate not only Jane but thousands of female readers who have read the novel in the nearly two centuries since Brontë penned it. The same could be said for Jane Austen's elusive Mr. Darcy. Brooding, arrogant, disagreeable. Yet one key attribute sets both men apart—and, I suspect, keeps the women who read about them yearning to encounter just such a man in real life: Inside, both Darcy and Rochester are deeply passionate souls, and in the course of their respective stories, they *step up to the plate and let their romantic feelings for the girl be known.* They arrive at a point in time where the ardor of their affections forces them to "declare themselves" to the girl or woman of their choosing. In short, *they pursue.*

There's something very attractive about being pursued with intent. In fact, several women in the survey cited this as a feature that might entice them to date someone. One woman in the 30–34 age range wrote in her survey response,

> Before my present boyfriend, I had a series of "confusing friendships" in which I spent a lot of time with certain guys, and there seemed to be mutual interest (there was on my part, at least, and I thought I recognized enough "signals" from the other end to hope it was), but those relationships ended up going nowhere. During these friendships, these guys and I would call each other, flirt, talk on the phone, seek each other out in social settings, spend one-on-one time together, and even be seen talking excessively at parties or other group gatherings to the point where people commented on it and thought we might be hanging out.
>
> I think a big part of what attracted me to my current boyfriend is that he actually had the guts to ask me out on a date, to make his interest known, and to pursue me. After over five years in a church young adult group, he's one of the only guys who have actually asked me out...I think guys need to buck up and ask girls out and not just rely on maybe seeing a girl at some church group event or whatever.

Pursuit—ah, that's it, really, when it all boils down to the essence of dating. As I scanned the responses from the women in my survey, I heard a repeated longing to be pursued, to be wooed, to be *won,* in the old-fashioned sense of the word. My mother's generation had another phrase for this courtship dance: "I chased him till he caught me." Is there a hint of coy flirtation in that phrase? You bet. Is there perhaps an implicit understanding that women have an active role to play in the chasing-and-catching dance? Absolutely. But at its core, this archaic statement speaks of what I simply call *longing.*

What is it that feeds this longing in women? The source is as ancient as the dawn of time, and the setting is the Garden of Eden. Listen to God's own words in Genesis:

> To the woman [God] said: "I will greatly
> multiply your sorrow and your conception;
> In pain you shall bring forth children;
> *Your desire shall be for your husband"*
> (3:16, emphasis added).

God was spelling out the terms of Eve's curse in this passage, her recompense for eating the forbidden fruit of the tree of the knowledge of good and evil. It's curious, isn't it, that desire for her husband should be listed among the punishments Eve had to suffer because of her sin. But when we read the second part of God's pronouncement, it makes better sense: "And he [your husband] shall rule over you."

Some theologians take a different stance on this passage. For me, it spells out—and makes sense of—the deep longing within woman for the love of a man, particularly the love of *one* special man. In essence, woman is *afflicted* with this desire. Indeed, writes Wendy Shalit in *A Return to Modesty*, most women prefer the love of one good man over the attentions of many men.

Shalit has hit on a nerve. The world may have moved on, become hip and high-tech and politically correct, but the old-fashioned values persist in our very makeup. We can't get away from who we are as women—created with a longing that goes deep. Some men may enjoy a season of sowing their wild oats and jockeying from one woman to the next, but it's rare to find a woman who actually prefers *multiple* men to one good one. So it's all the more frustrating when we see men we like and send them signals that we're interested (eye contact, lively conversation, hair flipping, flirting, etc.), but they do nothing. The frustration can even send well-meaning and sincerely searching Christian women to other wading pools beyond the one marked "Christian only."

As one female survey respondent noted, "I think men have contributed to the current marriage crisis by not taking the initiative to ask women out. I'm a Christian and would love to marry a Christian man one day, but they're just not stepping up. Honestly, I've considered dating outside my faith simply because the Christian dating pool seems sparse at best. It has to get better than this, right?"

All this talk about longing to be pursued begs the question: What does pursuit look like in the modern-day world, the real world we inhabit, not the one Jane Austen lived in?

The Dating Dance

What does pursuit look like in a world where formal pronouncements and calling cards have given way to text messages and MySpace referrals? Though many women long for the old-fashioned protocols, most don't honestly expect a man to show up on her doorstep in a cold-call appeal for love, bouquet in hand. In fact, it might be a little creepy. From talking to other women, I got the feeling that pursuit of *any kind* is preferable to a man sending "interested" signals and then never acting on them (excluding stalker tactics).

"It seems like Christian men are somehow either painfully awkward in the approach or painfully awkward in not approaching," writes one woman. "They're either way too forward in their approach (definite turnoff) or they hover forever, hoping maybe we'll take the lead. Non-Christian men just don't seem to have the inhibition most Christian men I've known seem to have, which is sad. I would just like Christian men to treat me like an attractive person they would like to get to know better, as opposed to either the elixir for their insecurities ('Please just say yes') or a long-term commitment if they ask me to coffee."

Perhaps the more awkward men could take cues from the following examples.

A young woman I know went to dinner with friends one night, and before they left, their waitress brought over a slip of paper. As she handed the paper to my friend, she said, "See that waiter over there? He's cute, right? Well, he wanted me to give this to you." She smiled and then left the table.

My friend unfolded the slip of paper and saw that it contained the guy's name and phone number. She couldn't stop talking about it all night. I asked her if she planned to call the guy, and she said yes.

Flattering? Yes. Creepy? No. The way this guy handled it was tactful and classy, showing genuine interest but putting the right of refusal (or reciprocation) into the girl's hands.

One time a man in a video store made eye contact with me. We both kept glancing at each other to the point where he approached me and casually asked if I had seen a particular movie and could I recommend it. It was a nice gesture and had a natural feel to it. We bantered for a few minutes and might have exchanged e-mails (a far safer first-communication medium than phone numbers, in my opinion), but my youngest daughter walked up right then, and the situation quickly turned awkward. I mumbled something like "Nice to meet you" and left the store knowing I would probably never see him again. His approach was flattering, not creepy, and later I could have kicked myself for leaving the store without exchanging some kind of contact information. One love-and-dating expert, who writes columns for Yahoo, recommends that single men and women keep a modern-day calling card for just such a purpose.

As to why so many singles struggle to find mates in the church, one woman wrote that the finger of blame goes both ways, but she went on to say that "men just don't seem to take the initiative anymore and are too worried about what everyone else will think/expect of any interest expressed in a woman (though, rightfully so in some cases, where people with good intentions meddle too much and say too much)." They're also too worried that a woman will immediately "expect the whole enchilada," she adds. Happily, she sees a positive trend in her own church: "I've now witnessed four young, early 20-something men buck that trend and take the initiative with intentional dating/marriage, and it was refreshing to watch. But it seems the problem is more in the 30- to 40-something cohort, the age group (male and female alike) that carries 'baggage,' from serial dating mishaps to divorce to children, and there's more hesitation to take even a first step."

Another woman addressed the "baggage" issue in her survey response, writing that "men have become complacent about putting forth the effort to do their part in having successful relationships. This means that they need to take ownership of their baggage, deal with it in a mature manner, let it go, and be willing to move forward by not holding new or potential partners back because of their past hurts," she writes. "They also need to cut the apron strings with their parents and be independent!"

Just Friends—or More?

Enough women in my survey mentioned guy *friends* they were interested in that it makes one Jane Austen scenario of particular interest for modern couples: the classic scene in *Emma* (the movie) between the main character and her friend/neighbor, Mr. Knightley, when he finally declares his love for her. Prior to this scene, Emma has awakened to her feelings for Mr. Knightley, clued in by her own fierce jealousy upon learning that her friend Harriet Smith has designs on him. About the same time, Knightley, who has always been attentive and *there* for Emma, decides to step up his game and make his intentions known to her: he wants to be more than her friend. The next time they meet, the scene is charged with raw emotion—a new, awkward awareness of love on Emma's part, and an eager attitude of entreaty on Knightley's. He begins to declare his love for her, but she stops him, thinking he is about to divulge his love for Harriet instead.

In typical comedy-of-errors fashion, they almost don't connect during this poignant love scene, but the audience knows these two are meant for each other. Finally Emma tells Mr. Knightley she was rude to cut him off, and anything he wishes to tell her, she will listen to with respect. Then Knightley says the unforgettable words, "Emma, you always want to keep me as your friend, but I hope someday to call you something much dearer than a friend." At that moment Emma realizes for the first time that her love for Mr. Knightley—her best friend—is actually reciprocated, and she may at last call him "*my* Mr. Knightley."

There's a sweetness to the scene that's hard to surpass in literature or on film. But the truly thrilling moment comes when Knightley finally breaks the barrier between friendship and romance by declaring his love for Emma. And, men, that's exactly what we women are longing for *you* to do with us, to let us know you're wanting to take the relationship to the next level. Granted, the situation can be tricky when it comes to letting a guy or girl *friend* know you're interested in much more than palling around for the rest of your life. Yet who wants to risk losing a potential mate just to save face? At some point, we all have to decide that a certain risk is worth the taking.

One female survey respondent had this to say about when the just-friends status goes on too long:

> Men complain that women don't "act" like women and let men lead. Maybe it's because it's been so long since we were treated like ladies, we've forgotten it would be really nice to be taken out to dinner and treated like a lady. However, I don't think that dating to be dating is good either. At this point in my life, time is short, and if I'm going on a date, it's because I have some thought that this person might be someone I want to be with long term. But so far I haven't had that problem because *no one* is asking me out anyway! They e-mail, text, call, and use that "I want to be friends with a woman first," which is good, but it also takes away the romance. I mean, I don't want a guy to come up after three years of friendship and say, you know, "I think we should date." I mean, what happened? Did he realize there was nothing

better or just get tired of looking and decide to settle? It would be nice if after a year or so of "friendship," he said, you know, "I've always been attracted to you." That would work, but I know girls who have been friends with a guy and dated on and off for years!

One woman cautioned that men need to be aware that any physical touch "might complicate the relationship they have with their female friends, especially if they have no intention of pursuing a dating relationship."

Over and over I heard the words, "I wish men would step up to the plate and take a risk in asking me out." Yet another woman lamented, "This 'I just want to be your Christian brother or friend' stuff isn't what women are looking for, and it confuses us to no end. You can pursue us and show us you're interested and still be respectful of us and our boundaries."

Ironically, single Christian men echoed the same "friend" complaint that many women voiced, but with a twist. While women complained that the men friends they want to be with won't "step up" (read: take the relationship beyond friendship to dating), men complained that many women *only* want to be friends when men show romantic interest in them. Much of this may be a classic case of unrequited love, but I wonder how many couples never get together simply because one person never finds the courage to tell the other that, like Mr. Knightley, he or she hopes someday to call the other much more than a friend.

Tips for Shy Guys

I'm tempted to think that the bolder men reading this don't need any cues for how to pursue a woman they like, but my single friend David tells me almost every guy has insecurities when it comes to women. So here goes. I informally polled a handful of single women friends, asking them how a man might let them know he's interested. Their list included the following:

- If you're in her network of online friends, establish rapport through e-mail or IM first, and then ask her to meet you for coffee. (Social networking sites like Facebook and MySpace make connecting easier, and you can "hide" behind the written word until you get a yes…or no.)

- If you have a mutual friend, let him or her know you're interested in an introduction with said person that includes the three of you. Believe me, you'll find out fast if she's interested too.

- If you know her phone number, send her a friendly—but ever-so-slightly flirty—text message.

- If you see her at a restaurant, ask the waiter serving her table to send over her favorite dessert (or drink), along with your name and phone number and/or e-mail address.

- If you work together, find ways to have casual conversations (near the water cooler, in the break room, working on projects together) until you break the ice. Then ask via e-mail if she'd like to go to lunch sometime—your treat.

Of course, there's no guarantee of success with any of these strategies, and they all still carry the risk of rejection, but trying and perhaps failing is better than never trying and surely failing. And the good news is, you just might be pleasantly surprised.

What Does Her Body Language Say?
I said earlier that pursuit is very attractive to a woman, and this can definitely be true. Sometimes guys who ordinarily wouldn't turn our heads suddenly get taken seriously when they show they're head over heels for us. However, overpursuit can be a turnoff, and the simplest

way to tell which "light" you're receiving—green light or red light—is to read our nonverbal cues. "Sure, no problem!" I can hear the men saying. "Women are already confusing enough, and now you want us to *read their minds?*" No, their bodies, actually. Body language is a surefire way to know what someone is thinking or feeling toward you, and once you grasp a few basic cues, you'll be better equipped to take their interest temperature—slightly chilly or a warming trend, freezing cold or smoking hot.

Here are some nonverbal cues that say, "Yes, I'm interested":

- She gazes into your eyes with deep interest, and her pupils are dilated.
- She raises both eyebrows exaggeratedly for a couple of seconds, combined with a smile and eye contact.
- She winks at you while talking to you or winks at you from a distance.
- While talking to you, she blinks more than usual, fluttering her eyelashes.
- Her smile reaches her eyes and looks natural and relaxed.
- She tilts her head.
- She plays with her hair while talking or listening to you (twirling a strand of hair, throwing her hair back off her shoulders, etc.).
- She fixes, pats, or smooths her outfit while talking to you.
- If her legs are crossed (while sitting), her upper leg is crossed toward you.
- She is turned toward you, whether sitting or standing.
- She plays with her jewelry.
- She touches your arm, shoulder, or hand while talking to you.

- She raises or lowers the volume of her voice to match yours.
- She speeds up or slows down her speaking to match yours.
- She laughs in unison with you.
- In a crowd, she speaks only to you and focuses her undivided attention on you.
- She mirrors your body language and body positions.

Here are some signs that say no:

- She never glances your way (across a room, in a crowd).
- She makes only fleeting eye contact.
- She looks away quickly, eyes level.
- Her posture is unchanged.
- She doesn't preen or play with her hair in any way.
- She turns her body away from you.
- Her head remains vertical, her eyes neutral.
- She maintains a neutral, polite expression.
- Her eyes appear normal or dull, no light.
- She keeps her mouth closed.

Finally, if you're a single guy who's looking for love in this lonely planet, I can offer you no better clue than the words of these and other real-world single women:

> "Men need to start being men. Women need them to step up to their role and be leaders/pursuers. Men need to be intentional with their actions and words. It seems like it's accepted for them to still act like little boys."

> "I just feel like men my age are complacent and not fun anymore... and they're looking for someone with a 20-year-old body."

"Don't casually, repetitively talk *about* marriage—only when you're about to propose. Many self-proclaimed Christian men don't exemplify true Christianity. They don't seem to know what they want or be honest about what they really want versus what they should want. Developing friendships first is important."

Guys need to ask girls out, to actually pursue.
There are so many wonderful Christian women
available, wanting to get married and start families.
But guys are being too passive.

"I think men put too much pressure on themselves about how they need to be...and what they need to be for a woman. Yes, as a woman, especially a Christian woman, I require or expect certain things, but I'm forgiving and not without grace, and I'm more than willing to share that grace and give it to someone else, especially in a relationship. I feel that men fear the unknown, and they often aren't willing to take the risk, even in dating, because of the pressures that surround them and the truth they've been taught by their church. If they would let their guards down, they would realize that a woman is ready to love them as they are...and hope for them the growth that only God can provide. I think that men fear leading and failing at it, then they don't lead at all. We as women also need to step up and *let* men lead. We become too independent and don't know how to let them lead properly or in the way we desire."

"A lot of single men want women to put forth most of the effort. They seem very caught up in their insecurity."

"I think many guys are waiting until their 30s to get married (which I think is great), but then they seem to be almost threatened by the women their age because the women have set up lives of their own, make good livings, and don't need a man to take care of them financially."

"I've learned that there is nothing I can do to force God's hand in this matter. I know there was a time when I blamed it on guys dropping the ball out of fear of failure. I know I've blamed other women who in their insecurity have played with men to feel better about themselves and then just left them broken and confused. In my case, the blame game had to stop, and I had to just accept God's plan for my life and trust Him to lead me to make the best decisions He wants me to make for my life. My decisions aren't what our culture says, and they aren't always what all Christians would do, but I have to make the ones God's leading me in. At the end of day, there's grace for the mistakes or the missed opportunities."

"I think that Christian men have contributed to the current marriage crisis by not taking the responsibility to grow up and be serious about choosing to date suitable Christian women and choosing to make the commitments they're so scared of making."

"I think many men are so complacent, self-centered, and passive that they believe they have no reason to ever get married. It's easier just to live their own lives by themselves than to take the risks of really growing up and becoming husbands and fathers."

"I think the stronger Christian men have been misinformed about women now. They think with all our women's lib, we don't want the romance of men being men and women being women. This is false. We want to be treated as equal but different."

"(1) I think we have to deal with the statistical fact that there are fewer Christian men than women. (2) I think we have to deal with passivity in men and aggressiveness in women. (3) I think we have to deal with some of the cultural lies about marriage we impose on Christian beliefs."

Take a risk and initiate with single women in your church. Be the man. Most Christian women are just waiting for a man to step up to the plate and ask. It doesn't have to be serious, but because dating is such a rarity, Christians tend to take the entire process too seriously. There are so many amazing Christian women who have yet to be really "seen" by the men who worship right next to them.

"God didn't create you to be passive...Pursuit seems to be obsolete, but we still want to be pursued. Don't give in to the pressure of dating only a certain type of woman. Believe it or not, the Lord is a lot more creative as to what He considers beautiful."

"Too many good men are just not dating at all. They seem to be afraid to risk. I feel like they *need* to work on their emotional stuff and move toward health and wholeness—emotional, spiritual, and physical wholeness."

"It seems like men aren't willing to take the risk of asking a woman out, since they don't have to anymore. There are plenty of women who will chase them, yet, I won't. I want them to pursue me. Also, a lot of men are way too focused on the externals—what a woman looks like or what a woman can do for them (cook, clean, add a lot of income to the family, etc.). I want to be loved and valued for who I am as a person and what I have to offer as a loving feminine companion."

"These days it seems that men in the church don't pursue women. All women want to feel desired and pursued, so we get frustrated when men don't step up! I've only been asked out by one guy from church since I moved to this state three years ago. I'm among many beautiful single women who are getting fed up with the men!"

---

*When my boyfriend and I first started talking,
we talked about the "wimpy" Christian guys who are out
there. The guys who are too "scared" to be bold in Christ
and ask girls out. Also, there are too many guys out there
who want to play the field. They don't want a committed
relationship. My boyfriend moved quickly to establish that
we were in a real relationship and not dating other people.
So many guys balk at this step, which is sad.*

"The Bible says that when a man finds a wife, he finds a good thing. Men, you need to step up. We aren't supposed to be in pursuit of you; you're meant to take the lead. This may seem old-fashioned, but it's biblical."

"Men, please don't be afraid to ask us out on a date. One date doesn't mean it's a serious relationship. And hanging out shouldn't last very long. If you like us, ask us out. Be brave! We like that more than you know."

"Quit saying, 'I'm waiting on God to bring me my future mate.' What a cop-out! You're scared, and you're afraid of being hurt or rejected and—*gasp!*—you might be tempted to have sex! I'm not scared. I wanted to date different kinds of people. I wanted to see what kinds of men I would be compatible with. I wanted to experience different social situations as part of a couple. I wanted to learn about myself in relationships. I'll soon be marrying a wonderful Christian man, but every other guy I've dated wasn't Christian. You so-called godly men never asked."

"We want to be pursued…we want men to ask, to seem interested."

"Guys need to ask girls out, to actually pursue. There are so many wonderful Christian women available, wanting to get married and start families. But guys are being too passive."

The message from single Christian women in the modern age couldn't be clearer: pursue us! And, as one woman added encouragingly, "Don't give up!"

9

"Guys Are Looking for a Supermodel with a Mother Teresa Personality"

(Men have unrealistic expectations • They demand perfection)

*Do you love me because I am beautiful,
or am I beautiful because you love me?*

CINDERELLA, IN ROGERS
AND HAMMERSTEIN'S CINDERELLA

We're all lovers of beauty and reward it our entire lives, even though politically correct protocol forbids us to admit this truth. Yet from the school yard to the career front to the arena of romantic love, the beautiful have a distinct advantage over the homely. "Ah, but beauty is in the eye of the beholder," you say. True enough, and thankfully we're not all clamoring to love the same man or woman; we're not all attracted to the same "look" in the mates we choose. But sometimes things feel out of balance, as if standards for beauty are being pushed beyond the reach of the average man or woman. What do we do then?

In my survey, the second most common frustration voiced by single Christian women about their male counterparts can be summed up in the statement "Men demand perfection." Not just in the beauty department, but in whole-person character and personality, it seems. The lament of one woman, already cited earlier in the book, bears repeating: "I think, generally, Christian men are looking for a Martha

Stewart, Mother Teresa, [and] Venus Williams in Jessica Simpson packaging. There is no meeting those standards, and in the meantime I just get older and older."

Another woman writes, "I don't know if the media's feeding them this idea that as Christian men they have a right to expect a woman who is both drop-dead beautiful and has a fantastic personality. Not that it has to be one or the other, but it almost seems as if they feel that since they're Christians they're entitled to only the best."

So many Christian guys are looking for "a supermodel with the heart of Mother Teresa" and are so picky, writes one female respondent, "that they bypass amazing women right in front of them for some ideal that I'm not sure even exists." To be fair, however, she admits, "I know women tend to do the same thing." And in fact the same complaint has a polar opposite. She also observes that in the young-adult groups she's been a part of, "there are a plethora of amazing, independent, interesting, and attractive women and a plethora of men who have poor social skills and who don't measure up to what a lot of women want...All the girls are interested in maybe two or three guys, and those guys don't date anyone until a new young girl comes along whom all the guys want to date. Not that I have any opinions on this."

In the "What Men Say..." section of this book, we'll take a look at the issue of beauty, or lack of it (including the issue of weight), from the male perspective. The twist here, from the women's viewpoint, is that men are so demanding, women can't possibly meet their standards of perfection.

Size Does Matter

A few years ago, a quiet transition took place in my life as a woman: I became invisible. Some of the women reading this book may already know what I'm talking about. This phenomenon, I'm discovering, is horribly common among the female half of the species. So much so that the mere mention of it can bring tears to a woman's eyes.

My invisibility had nothing to do with the lack of a pretty face or a lively personality, but it had everything to do with a formidable acronym called BMI (body mass index). Following my exodus from the corporate world several years ago, I gradually packed on 25 extra pounds that wouldn't seem to budge, no matter what I did. No, it didn't put me in the obese category, but it did render me *invisible* to the majority of men I encountered—at least in the state I call home, where golden tans and stick-thin bodies are the high-water mark of beauty, a place where standards for female beauty are more demanding, I suspect, than in, say, Iowa or South Dakota. I finally got fed up with this chunkier version of myself and lost the weight, and so it's easier for me to write about it now in hindsight.

Our modern culture can be cruel, especially when it renders attractive women invisible to an opposite-sex world conditioned to Hollywood standards of beauty. This gradual entry into invisible status seemed especially harsh because I had always enjoyed a reasonable amount of male attention, the kind every woman secretly yearns for: sideways glances on the street, a man tripping over himself to hold a door for you, random eye contact with a smile. Was I now undesirable?

I discovered I wasn't alone in this predicament, not by any means. When I mentioned the "invisible" phenomenon to one friend, she nodded her head slowly. "I know what you mean," she said, her voice suddenly husky as she looked away.

Another friend could relate too. Over dinner one night, we discussed the invisible phenomenon, and sure enough, tears sprang to her eyes.

"After a while you just get used to it," she said. "You stop expecting it."

"Expecting what?" I asked.

"Expecting to be looked at."

Imagine our surprise when we took a trip to the North Carolina mountains that fall and caught several men looking our way.

"Kathy, did you see that?" I whispered as we made our way into a movie theater ticket line. "That man positively *stared* at you!"

She smiled and told me she had noticed. The same thing happened to me. We both chalked it up to easier standards on women in this part of the country, and men who actually *like* curves, God bless 'em. But we didn't live in western North Carolina, or some other part of the country where the standards of beauty are less strict than in the "glamour" states.

Driving back to our hotel, we couldn't stop talking about what had happened at the theater. Later we found proof in an article about differing standards of female beauty. It included a quote from a man in (you guessed it) western North Carolina, who said his mountain brothers appreciated women with curves—even those a few pounds overweight. I told Kathy that I was considering a move to the mountains.

Seriously, as Christians we all know that inward beauty is of more value than the outward appearance. Women are encouraged to cultivate the quiet beauty that comes from a life of purity and devotion to God. I agree wholeheartedly with all of those things, but at the same time, you and I live in the real world. Show me a single flesh-and-blood woman who doesn't long to be beautiful, and I'll show you a world that grades on a curve (hint: it doesn't). Whether or not we admit it, God placed inside us a desire to be desirable. Remember, it's right there in Genesis: "Your desire shall be for your husband" (3:16). That ancient longing to be noticed and adored by a man. And there's no denying that physical attraction is usually the first thing that draws two people together.

A young woman I know took an art-history trip to Europe over the summer with a group of fellow college students. When they got back, everyone had stories to tell. I heard about freezing atop the Eiffel Tower in a drizzly cold rain, rude Parisians, four-course Italian meals that seemed to go on forever, frescoes so magnificent they took their breath away seeing them up close, the palpable feeling they got standing in the Oracle at Delphi, being swarmed by overfriendly pigeons in St. Mark's Square, the backdrop of Venice looking like a stage set all around them. Among the colorful stories they told, a single theme kept cropping up from several of the girls. "You know, here at home a lot of people consider me overweight," one young woman said, "but the Mediterranean men couldn't keep their eyes off me. In Italy and Greece, I'm a total hottie!"

I'm thankful for celebrities and other role models who are working to change pop-culture standards of beauty so they're more reasonable. I'm grateful to the sisterhood of women who love and accept one another despite our myriad foibles and failings. I'm thankful for the men out there who do find voluptuous curves wildly attractive (need I remind anyone what Rubens models and other Renaissance beauties looked like?). And I *am* grateful to God for shining His light into the hearts of men and women, giving them a beauty that glows from the inside out.

I've grown philosophical about this whole invisibility thing. People change, times change, and standards change. Yes, some women need to take a good, hard look in the mirror and admit they've let themselves go—and it's time to do something about it. There *is* a point where "a few extra pounds" turns into obesity. Maybe you could wear more stylish clothes or fix your hair in a more flattering style. Perhaps you need a little makeup or need to tone down the makeup you're already wearing. If you're brave, you could ask a male friend with a kind heart to give you an honest assessment, suggesting things you might do to improve your "street appeal."

As for men, I encourage you to wean your eyes from impossible standards of perfection and retrain them to see "real" women, to really notice them again. Maybe you've secretly fed on a diet of airbrushed, silicone-enhanced images and forgotten what real bodies and faces look like. Maybe you need to travel to a different area on vacation and notice how much the prevalent standard of female beauty in your area affects men and women alike. (You don't need to leave the country to observe this—regional differences will suffice and give you all the evidence you need.)

For some men, the problem isn't a lack of attraction for women the culture deems overweight or not pretty enough; it's the peer pressure they experience from what *other men* say about these women. As one woman wrote in my survey, the need to pursue "only skinny women that the culture espouses as beautiful" is a huge pressure for both men and women. "A man won't date a woman he is attracted to because he fears others' disapproval," she writes. "There are lots of beautiful women out there who don't have the same measurements as a *Playboy* centerfold."

The words of another survey participant sum up well what women think about this issue of beauty and perfection. She writes,

> I think that everyone has the picture of the perfect ideal person, and usually that's a fairy tale. The attributes they're looking for aren't attainable. Some of them—in and of themselves—might be, but for one person to have all of them isn't realistic. We also like to base things on how we feel rather than on godly characteristics. Most of the dating relationships I've had with men, when I felt the "warm-fuzzy" feelings, weren't based on anything other than emotions. It's the relationships that are based on character and who a person really is that last. If men could understand this, it might help with the problems of bypassing suitable mates and delayed marriages.

Listen to what other women have to say about beauty:

> "Part of it is being scared, and part of it is that there seems to be some sense of entitlement among Christian men—that God is going to bless them with a Barbie wife, and they shouldn't have to settle. It's stupid."

I hate to see Christian men looking for the same thing as
non-Christians...mainly young, hot, and ready to serve.

"Men are unwilling to really explore their own role in the per-ceived problem of undatable women. I feel like they don't give women a chance. Like men think they know what's attractive to them (based on all of society's messages), when in fact they may be attracted to a *much* wider range of women. But they don't give women a chance."

"A lot of times, guys seem even more picky when it comes to appearance in the Christian dating scene. It seems they have this idea that they tell God exactly what they want their wife to look like, and then they only date girls that fit into that box, and they miss out on others who are attractive not only physi-cally but in much deeper ways."

"I'm not sure being single constitutes a crisis! But men certainly seem to be stuck on a look or a type that's very limiting."

"I feel a lot of guys out there are only looking for trophy women. Perhaps I may not look like a supermodel on the outside, but I know that once you get to know me, you would love me. Take the time to get to know someone before you judge them. Of course, you have to be attracted to the person you're dating, but quit looking for a supermodel...unless, of course, that's the number-one thing on your list."

"Take the time to get to know people. Don't limit yourself to that picture in your head of what you think you want. You may be pleasantly surprised."

"Christian men seem to be almost worse than nonsaved men when it comes to full-figured women. They see the pretty face, yet think, *Oh, if they would only lose weight.* They can't get past the exterior. Yet when you ask them, they say that beauty comes from the soul. But they won't even take the time to get to know the soul behind the full-figured woman. There are lots of double standards here."

"I guess men have bought into the myth that they can have it all. They also have unrealistic expectations."

"I think the problem is that men are seeking perfection and avoiding personal spiritual growth. Rather than choosing a mate to grow with, many of the opposite sex seem to want the perfect mate while simultaneously ignoring their own faults. The same religious-compatibility issues that have splintered the body of Christ into scores of denominations are also keeping marriageable Christians from pursuing serious relationships with each other."

"I think both men and women need to learn to look beyond the surface. I think it's still too much about looks, finances, and success as modern society defines it, which, while these factors do play an important role in a relationship, they shouldn't be the defining qualities someone looks for in a future mate."

10

"ALL THE GOOD ONES ARE TAKEN"

(There aren't enough single men to go around)

Almost every single woman I know past the age of 35 will say these words when the topic of marriage comes up, and specifically, when asked why they can't find a man to marry: "All the good ones are taken." The sad truth is they say it with all sincerity.

"Because single women often outnumber single men in the church, men usually have all the advantages. Women get stuck with whatever is left over," decries one woman who responded to my singles survey. But that's not the end of her frustration: "And because most single Christian women I know are rather old-fashioned in their thinking, we don't want to make the first move. So we also have no control over who asks us out and when."

If there ever was a cliché among the single set, it's this: *All the good ones are taken!* Ironically, single Christian men voiced a similar complaint, lamenting the lack of availability among single women (implied: women who aren't already dating or married), while women bemoan the lack of "good ones" still on the market. This subtle but key difference hints that women may actually be pickier when it comes to choosing mates, although the common female hue and cry charges men with exacting impossible standards (see the previous "supermodel" chapter).

John Molloy recounts in his book *Why Men Marry Some Women and Not Others* that for older single women, "All the good ones are taken" is the second biggest complaint. (The number-one complaint is "It's hard to meet eligible men.") But he doesn't let them off easily. The real problem older single women face in developing relationships with men is that they're "still looking at men the way they did in high school," he writes. Back then, the ideal man was the star football player or other champion athlete. The cold reality, he asserts, is that women continue to pursue men who are tall, good-looking, and with a full head of hair, but often that's not what the singles landscape is filled with once you're over 40. Molloy goes on to say,

> Women are constantly complaining about men being shallow; they gripe about men being interested only in how a woman looks and claim that's why many men in their forties and fifties go after twenty-year-olds. In fact, many women turn down older men for similar reasons. The men don't fit the picture they developed in high school or in their twenties of the ideal husband...When this subject was brought up, women always denied a man's looks played such an important part in their decision making. But when we asked them whether they would date a man several inches shorter than they, or one who had a lisp, most admitted they might have a problem with either.[1]

A subset of this complaint goes something like this: "When men do decide to date or marry, they often choose women 10 to 15 years younger." Unfortunately, there's an awful lot of truth to this complaint women lobbed against the single men they meet. Both statistically and circumstantially, you can see the veracity of this claim played out again and again. In his characteristic hard-hitting way Molloy writes,

"Don't make the mistake of thinking there are still many men available just because you see men wandering around unmarried in their late thirties and early forties. Scores of women who reached thirty-six told us the men they knew in that age range were dating and marrying women in their twenties."[2]

However, most people end up marrying someone close to their own age, Molloy states, and women who widen their social circles and *make friends with other women* are often the first ones to head to the marriage-license bureau. Why friends with other women? Because, Molloy attests, single women with lots of single female friends tend to help one another out, setting each other up on blind dates and socializing together in places where single men congregate. In short, they support one another in this common endeavor, all within the context of a genuine friendship.

In talking with single Christian women, I discovered two offshoot trends of this complaint against Christian men: (1) women started to look seriously at non-Christian men who were otherwise good, moral individuals, and (2) an increasing number of older women who keep themselves attractive and fit are dating much younger men—as much as 15 years younger (an ironic twist of fate perhaps?). Seen through the impartial lens of supply and demand, this second trend makes good sense. Since there are fewer eligible men in their 40s, and it's so much harder to meet them, women who retain their youthful beauty can fish in the much larger pool of younger single men. Or, as the case may be (especially on Internet dating sites), the younger men find them.

One woman recounted her own dating adventures with a much younger man. She found to her surprise that they were extremely compatible, and she came to regard him as her best friend. "After a while the lines between your ages blur and you start to see him as just the person he is, not simply as a younger guy," she said. In her case, a crossroads came when she was ready to move toward marriage, but her friend wasn't. He loved her, he said, but he realized he was still years away from being ready for that level of commitment. That's not the case for every younger man, however. I heard not long ago that the friend of a friend is engaged to be married—she's 50 years old; he's 35.

As Shakespeare wrote, "All's fair in love and war." As to the idea of men pursuing much-younger women, one respondent wrote, "I believe once a man reaches his 40s, he won't consider marrying a woman his same age. I believe if Christian men are considering marriage, they should choose a mate to date exclusively once they reach the age of 25."

"Why are all the 30-something guys finally settling down and choosing 20-something girls?" lamented another. "There are lots of wonderful, fun Christian women in their 30s looking for guys of similar faith."

And finally: "Bypassing suitable mates, *yes!* What do I know about any marriage crisis?"

As with any social-behavior-versus-perception issue, we may never know which gender *really* suffers the most from a lack of suitable mates. And John Molloy's contention that women are guilty of being too picky does hold water. But the responses from women on this subject sure makes a loud case for their side of the argument:

> "Where are the single Christian men?! In my church there are five women for every single man! And of those men, most seem passive and uninterested in pursuing women."

> "In the secular community, it's hard to find a man I can feel comfortable with, who wants the same things I do. In the Christian pool, either they're already married or they're not compatible. I'm not saying I would blame that on the opposite sex, but I'm starting to hope for a good Christian man who is married with no children and whose wife leaves him."

In the Christian pool, either they're already married or
they're not compatible. I'm starting to hope for a good
Christian man who is married with no children and
whose wife leaves him.

"I think sometimes the guys marry too soon because they know they're not to have sex before they're married, and they just can't wait, so they marry young. Then us girls who are older have a hard time even finding single guys in our age group who aren't already divorced or married."

"Well, in my opinion, it seems rare to find a single, *mature,* stable guy these days."

"Men Today Are Emotionally and Spiritually Immature and Take Too Long to Grow Up"

(Many men are intimidated by successful women)

This complaint proved to be almost as much of a hot-button issue as the complaint that men won't step up to the plate. In many ways, it's a different spin on the same issue, but the women who logged their frustrations regarding male immaturity were very specific, using phrases like "take too long to grow up" and "spiritually immature." Some women lay the blame on a culture that not only influences men to stay boys longer but actually coddles and rewards them for such behavior.

This was the conviction of one woman respondent, who wrote, "Men have been raised by a society that didn't give them the skills to be godly leaders and the warriors they were meant to be. Therefore, they are insecure and not able to see how deeply in need of healing they are. They won't commit for fear that they might get hurt or have their egos damaged further."

Another variation on this theme is that many single men are intimidated by successful single women and simply "don't know what to do with them." "Why are women who pursue careers or professions in the world viewed as less marriageable to strong Christian men?" stormed one female survey respondent. "We share a deep faith and calling to do what we do, and we want a strong Christian male with confidence whom we can support and who wants to support us. We like to collaborate on projects that we can both do, and share information, and share raising children, especially since both parents should be involved. We want to be considered partners as much as traditional stay-at-home women are. And yet we want men to embody certain traditional views, where they can be stronger and confident, so we don't always have to be independent."

Extended Adolescence?

I have to agree with the women who leveled this complaint against men, and it seems we're not the only ones who feel this way. The phenomenon of delayed male maturity is so prevalent, a new phrase was coined to capture it: extended adolescence. And it's not just happening to North American males. Experts have noted a disturbing trend toward elongated boyhood across the Atlantic too—a trend that often persists well into a man's 30s and beyond. In a Weblog titled "Extended Male Adolescence—the British Version," Albert Mohler, noted columnist and speaker, and president of the Southern Baptist Theological Seminary, states,

> *The Sunday Times* [London] reports that young British men are turning into "eternal bachelors" and the nation is turning into a "bachelor nation." In fact, men are…now marrying at a rate lower than at any time other than the most intense years of World War II. It's not that they are not having sex—they are just not making commitments.
>
> These young men are not even cohabitating—they are just living like irresponsible teenagers. As the newspaper reported, "While the fall in marriage is well documented, it has widely been thought this is because couples are moving in together instead. But the LSE

[London School of Economics] study, designed to test this notion, found growing numbers of men are simply not forming serious relationships until later in life."

In other words, they are not growing up. A civilization that fails to encourage its young men to accept adult roles and adult responsibilities—especially the responsibility of marriage—is sowing the seeds of its own destruction.[1]

In a cover story for *Time* magazine, Lev Grossman noted that our culture has produced a curious generation of young adults he calls "twixters," who are unlike any generation before them. "Social scientists are starting to realize that a permanent shift has taken place in the way we live our lives," writes Grossman. "In the past, people moved from childhood to adolescence and from adolescence to adulthood, but today there is a new, intermediate phase along the way. The years from 18 until 25 and even beyond have become a distinct and separate life stage, a strange, transitional never-never land between adolescence and adulthood in which people stall for a few extra years, putting off the iron cage of adult responsibility that constantly threatens to crash down on them. They're betwixt and between."[2]

Grossman adds that while "some of the sociologists, psychologists and demographers who study this new life stage see it as a good thing... more historically and economically minded scholars see it differently. They are worried that twixters aren't growing up because they can't. Those researchers fear that whatever cultural machinery used to turn kids into grownups has broken down, that society no longer provides young people with the moral backbone and the financial wherewithal to take their rightful places in the adult world. Could growing up be harder than it used to be?" Grossman cites a statistic from Bob Schoeni, a professor of economics and public policy at the University of Michigan, who stated that "the percentage of 26-year-olds living with their parents has nearly doubled since 1970, from 11% to 20%."[3]

A lot of twixters cite *Garden State* as one movie that really captures their predicament on-screen, Grossman reports. He quotes Zach Braff of *Scrubs* fame, then 29, who wrote, directed, and starred in the film, which features a 20-something actor who finally returns home after nine years away: "I feel like my generation is waiting longer and longer to get married," says Braff. "In the past, people got married and got a job and had kids, but now there's a new 10 years that people are using to try and find out what kind of life they want to lead. For a lot of people, the weight of all the possibility is overwhelming."[4]

Not surprisingly, the mind-set that fuels the twixters—who, by all indications now reach well into their 30s—is one that says, "Weddings can wait," writes Grossman. "Thirty is no longer the looming deadline it once was. In fact, five of the Chicago six see marriage as a decidedly post-30 milestone.

" 'It's a long way down the road,' says Marcus Jones, 28, a comedian who works at Banana Republic by day. 'I'm too self-involved. I don't want to bring that into a relationship now.' He expects to get married in his mid- to late 30s. 'My [future] wife is currently a sophomore in high school,' he jokes."[5]

Dr. Laura Schlessinger states bluntly in *Ten Stupid Things Men Do to Mess Up Their Lives* that "a terrible thing has happened to our culture. Growing in intensity since the 1960s, it is the supremacy of personal fulfillment and gratification over notions of obligation and commitment."[6] The net result, she sums up, is that many men feel "entitled" to happiness and the pursuit of their own satisfactions, even if it comes at the costly expense of abandoning commitments and obligations.

As one guy friend said to me, "I want a wife to come home to, I just don't want to have to come home."

This is toddler thinking, the mind-set that presupposes, "I am the center of the universe" and "It's all about me." In all honesty, sometimes it feels as if the available men left on the market are the poster boys for this mantra, the ones who shirked commitment and responsibility (read: marriage) in favor of endless boyhood. One woman who responded to my survey remarked on this tendency—and the shocking comment from a guy friend, whose words capture the extended-adolescent mind-set:

> It seems like the responsible Christian men look for wives in college and get married then or right after. Otherwise, it seems like Christian men have lost any sense of responsibility and what it takes to actually maintain a marriage relationship. As one guy friend said to me, *"I want a wife to come home to, I just don't want to have to come home."* It seems that a lot of men have accepted the selfishness that comes with the consumerism of our society and don't even realize it. They're also thoroughly intimidated by intelligent women, leaving those of us who refuse to abandon God's calling on our lives stranded as "impressive and attractive—for someone else." A greeting card: "Women would rather be beautiful than intelligent, because men can see better than they can think."

However you want to dice it, the single women who answered my survey have strong feelings about men who refuse to grow up and be *men*—and a big part of stepping into manhood, they reason, is taking on the commitment and responsibility of marriage. Reading their responses, it's easy to see that women find maturity very attractive in a man. If that's not reason enough for men to grow up as well as step up, I don't know what is.

Here's what other women had to say on the issue:

"Guys are less willing to grow up these days and settle down."

"Men today lack values and don't take responsibility."

"I think for many young adults, by the time they figure out what they want in a person, too much time has gone by, and the selection is less. It's also frustrating for us girls, who are especially taught in the church not to pursue but to sit back and wait for the guys around us to grow up when we've been ready a long time."

"Actually, I don't fault the opposite sex as much as I fault my own. In wanting everything, women have lost one of the most beautiful gifts available to them—being wives and mothers. But to answer the question, I think men have contributed to the current marriage crisis by a general immaturity. Men in their early 20s who are physically ready for marriage, aren't emotionally ready. By the time they are ready, somewhere between 30 and 40, the women are in their 30s as well, single and childless, having had to compromise or wonder if they will ever experience a husband and children."

"I think our parents are to blame. They made life so good for us. Women were raised to be independent, and now many think they don't need a man, and men have been spoiled and taught they don't need to grow up until they're at least 30! So women go out and build their own lives without men while the men live with their parents until they're 30."

"It's incredibly difficult and frustrating to be a Christian woman wanting to find a Christian spouse, especially when the Christian men around me are immature and nowhere near making a commitment in life."

Grow up and quit opting out of
relationships when they get hard.

"Grow up and quit opting out of relationships when they get hard. And *stop* saying you're looking for a Proverbs 31 woman when you're really looking for a housewife—that woman in Proverbs owns and runs at least one business, if not more; is the breadwinner for the family (literally); and is clearly doing more than being a housewife. If you're looking for a stay-at-home woman, that's fine, but don't blame it on Proverbs 31."

"Men want to play the field, or have their cake and eat it too"

(The candy-shop mindset • Too many choices—
why settle for this one when something better might come along?)

As dating options increase, so does choosiness—and the incumbent indecisiveness that goes along with it. Most people think of unlimited choices as a good thing, but as already mentioned in chapter 5, the idea that something better might perpetually be "just around the corner" works against you in the end. That very mentality—the existence of a candy shop of attractive single women to choose from—has tempted many men to hold out for the proverbial "something better." In doing so, women complain, men bypass some very worthy potential mates right under their noses.

"I think many guys think that if they take what they see in front of them, they may miss out on someone else down the line who would be better," wrote one woman in her survey response. "They see what we see, and that is that there are many singles out there."

A young woman I know shared her own bittersweet story of what it's like loving someone who's not quite sure he loves you *enough*—and tries to have his cake and eat it too. Gwen and David had dated for two and a half years when they decided to take a little break from each other and get some much-needed breathing room. "We loved each other very much but were starting to bicker over little things, get on each other's nerves, so a minibreak seemed like a good idea," says

Gwen. Once the couple spent time apart, however, they realized how much they missed each other and made plans to have dinner to catch up. That evening over sushi, David told Gwen how he'd met someone in a civic-theater group he'd joined. The catch? He wanted to date both of them, and he hoped Gwen would be open-minded about it.

"I feel like the past two and a half years we spent together meant nothing," says Gwen, her eyes wistful. "I mean, this is someone who said he *loved me,* and still does. He just wants me to make room in 'our' life for this third wheel."

Some guys aren't that obvious about it, thank goodness, but the attitude still abounds today.

The World at Our Fingertips

Singles pastor Brad Goad believes the self-serving consumerism mind-set that pervades the culture at large has changed the landscape of dating, even in the church. And he ought to know. Every week he oversees a ministry that caters to 600 single adults in the greater Houston area. "Culturally we've become much more independent and self-sustaining," says Goad. "And we don't have to interact on a personal basis as much as we used to, because we have the world at our fingertips. For those who are introverted and awkward, it's become a very difficult world, but for those who are competent in this new arena, there's no struggle. There's a greater tolerance overall for singleness today. There's not that inferiority of 'Gosh you're single.'"

The generation that grew up in the 70s and 80s, especially, grew up in a much more self-focused culture than their parents, says Goad, and that may explain why so many people approach romance with a "What's in it for me?" motive. "Think about it," he says. "Gone are the days when a company took care of you until retirement. You have to take care of yourself now. People look out for themselves now and not the individual—as opposed to 'How can I help grow this company, how can I stay in this city and get active in it, how can I be a part of this relationship?' From working with hundreds of singles, I see a window of time that when you bypass it—from your early to mid-20s—without getting married, you become more independent and transient. A lot of the people here [in Houston] have been transferred here, and they can easily move every two or three years with their company and not have to worry about a wife or kids. It's almost a self-perpetuating lifestyle. You become more self-sufficient at this stage. If you get married in college, you and your wife make those changes together. But if you get married later, you have to merge two lives, two careers."

Media Malediction

For some, it's obviously easier just to dispense with the hassle of romance and dating, not to mention the pursuit of marriage. And it's impossible to dismiss the media's heavy-handed influence on modern singles in this regard. The messages sent by movies and popular TV shows are decidedly antimarriage and paint the single life as carefree, exciting, and definitely something to be protracted as long as possible.

In a chapter called "Wedded Dis," author Jillian Straus *(Unhooked Generation)* writes, "Some very powerful scripts, of course, that influence many Gen-Xers, consciously or not, are the ones written by movie and television producers in Hollywood. To a remarkable degree, especially given the cliché that Hollywood's happy ending has always been matrimonial, many of the films and TV programs that are hits for this generation carry the not-so-subtle message that marriage is boring and single life is sexy."[1]

With shows such as *Seinfeld, Friends,* and *Sex and the City* as a cultural backdrop, the generation looking for love as frustrated singles today couldn't help but consume a diet of antimarriage sentiment. Compared to our parents' generation—who grew up with television shows like *I Love Lucy* and *Leave It to Beaver*—it's easy to see why regard for marriage has plummeted, especially for the male half of the species.

Straus describes overhearing a group of men—two married with children and two single—talk about their 40-something bachelor co-worker: "He still goes out and parties. He has the best life," they noted. Straus, in turn, notes, "Whether or not those remarks reflect men's true feelings, clearly it is an increasing social norm to be jealous of the single guy—or say that you are jealous."[2]

But Straus was reporting on secular culture, not singles within the church, you might say. True enough, and one might hope that *Christian* single men (and women) would be set apart from the cultural norms that guide behavior for the rest of society. However, in hearing women's responses on this subject, I discovered that too many found single Christian men following the same script as their unchurched brothers. As one woman wrote in my survey, "Our society has devalued marriage and the sanctity of the commitment that comes with it. Also the breakdown of families teaches new generations that marriage isn't really a serious institution, and whenever you grow tired of it or experience bumps in the road, you should just give up. This leads people in their search for a mate to just look at the here and now rather than looking deeper into the future."

Another woman in the 25–29 age range, and never married, concurred: "I believe that most men don't want to let their single life go. They want the best of both worlds. This could be said of both sexes, but it's usually expected of men to sow wild oats and for women to patiently wait until the man comes around."

The influence of what Straus calls "the cult of I" can lead today's singles to "develop the inner inclination to believe that we will be able to schedule love for whenever we're ready for it, and that it shouldn't involve much personal sacrifice. It can also result in a 'What have you done for me lately?' attitude in relationships."[3]

No doubt this type of thinking goes along with the male tendency to want to play the field. In a desperate attempt to avoid settling, many men raise their expectations to impossibly high standards, thinking it will help them weed out unsatisfactory women and narrow the field of possibilities. The unexpected irony is that it also narrows the likelihood of finding true love, as we'll see later.

As with so many of the themes that cropped up in my survey, some men had the same complaint against women, which we will discuss in part 3. Following are several other responses women shared on their survey results:

> "Men say that they want 'godly women,' yet they also want women who have 'worldly' standards. This happens no matter the age."

> "Some guys are always looking for something better."

> "Men don't want commitment. Women provide men with everything they need without marriage. Why would a man feel the need to commit or get married?"

> "Men have been gladly taking what we women have given them—sex with no strings attached and the luxury of putting off marriage."

"TOO Many christian Men try to push sexual Boundaries"

(They expect sex to be part of dating)

An attractive woman in her 40s, Laura was thrilled when she finally met a handsome man on a Christian dating Web site, and the connection seemed genuine. Of course, they had yet to meet in person, but all the signs pointed to a yes with this one. He made biblical allusions in his e-mails, talked about God's influence in his life, and told her about a Christian book he was writing, so she knew he was the real deal—not a poser trying to lure "good girls" online. The only obstacle was distance. Tom lived about 1,500 miles away, but what was distance when you really clicked with someone? He made it clear that he was willing to travel—or fly her up to his city—when the time was right.

After e-mailing for a while, Tom relocated to a new city, and his contact with Laura gradually dropped off. They lapsed into pen-pal status, checking in with each other every once in a while until the length of time between e-mails stretched into months. The last Laura heard, Tom had met someone special in his new city and was dating her. She was happy for him and felt little disappointment because, after all, they had never met, and so neither had invested their hearts. Meanwhile, Laura started dating someone in her own city.

Time passed, and one week after Laura's boyfriend broke up with her the following summer, she got a phone call from Tom out of the blue. Her broken heart was still aching, but Tom's easy humor and lighthearted conversation was just the elixir she needed. It was good to talk to her old friend again, and she couldn't believe God's good timing in bringing him back into her life at just the right moment. They talked on the phone almost every day for a week. Tom let her know he was back living in his old city again, free of relationship entanglements. He told her how much he would like to finally meet her in person, and when Laura concurred, he offered to fly her up and show her his beautiful city. "You can stay at the home of my boss and his wife. They have a huge house with several spare bedrooms," he said. "You'll love them. They're like family to me."

Laura agreed and made plans to meet Tom in two weeks' time. Two days later, before he had actually purchased her plane ticket, Tom talked to Laura again by phone, outlining all the fun activities he had planned for their weekend. Toward the end of the conversation he casually dropped, "So, are you okay with staying at my house over the weekend?"

This caught Laura off guard. "I thought you said I could stay with your boss' family," she stammered. "Tom, you know I like you very much, but you're still someone I've never met before, and you're a *man*. I'm really not comfortable staying at your house. Let's just continue with our original arrangements, okay?"

He said he understood and bantered with her for another few minutes. Later that evening, wanting to share some news with Tom, Laura dialed his cell phone. When he picked up, he didn't seem to recognize who had called, as if she were no longer programmed into his cell phone (and he had presumably forgotten her number). When she said, "It's me...Laura," he seemed to cheer up. They talked for a little while until he said he had to go.

A day passed with no word from Tom, who had previously been calling her as much as twice a day. When Laura again tried to call his number, all she got was his voice mail.

Gradually, as the next few days passed with no word from Tom—and no further word about her trip to see him—Laura got the hint loud and clear: once he realized he wasn't going to "get some" during his weekend with Laura, he lost interest and dropped off the face of the earth. She e-mailed him, telling him of her disappointment in his bait-and-switch move and his obvious motive for flying her up to see him. Of course, he never responded.

Sadly, Laura's story isn't as rare as you might expect among the Christian singles scene. And it wasn't the only time it happened to Laura. Another man from the very same Christian dating site later propositioned her outright and offered to fly down for a "date" (wink, wink) that weekend. She reported him to the Web site officials, getting his profile banned from the site.

Of course, online dating is one thing, and many women have come to expect an ulterior motive lurking behind those charming male profiles. But when you meet someone the old-fashioned way (through church events, family or friends, or other social settings) and get to know them gradually, it can come as a shock when a man suddenly pushes for sex.

"Most men my age claim to be Christians but are okay with pre-marital sex, which is absolutely ludicrous if you truly believe in God and the teachings of the Bible," said one never-married woman in her early 30s. Another woman who responded to my survey complained that "Christian men are a lot like non-Christians in that they don't always respect boundaries." And that's not the only problem, she stated. Christian men aren't into "growing together spiritually" and don't seem to realize that Christian women still want to be romanced (notes, flowers, open communication).

"I think way too many Christian men are living like non-Christians," said another woman in her mid-40s, who has also never married but wants to. "They expect sexual involvement to be a part of dating, or they escape from having to engage with a real woman and retreat into pornography. Also, I think a lot of fathers of boys are absent from their lives, so they grow up having no clue what it means to be a good man or to pursue a good woman."

On the flip side, one woman wrote that she thinks "sometimes guys marry too soon because they know they're not to have sex before they are married, and they just can't wait, so they marry young." Actually, her theory is backed up by solid research. The Barna Group reports that men tend to drop out of church earlier than women do, and this most definitely includes single men. Yet even among those single Christian men who do remain in circulation in church settings, many women report ulterior motives. Says one, "Men say that they want 'godly women,' yet they also want women who have 'worldly' standards. This happens no matter the age."

Of course, Christian women aren't an entirely innocent lot either, as we'll see in the next section. Many men decry the loss of virtue among the very women they look to as potential mates. But the first and most important complaint men leveled against women—by sheer number of responses on this theme—heads the list: men feel too much pressure from women to be spiritual giants.

PART 3

wHaT men say...

"Women expect too much from us (spiritually)—Real men are rough around the edges"

(Women are looking for spiritual giants • Women put too much pressure on men during a first date)

*It is in vain to say human beings ought to be
satisfied with tranquillity: they must have action;
and they will make it if they cannot find it.*

CHARLOTTE BRONTË, JANE EYRE

Just as women have one leading hot-button issue with single men—that they need to "step up to the plate"—so too have men with women: that the Christian women they see around them "expect too much" of them and have ridiculously high *spiritual* standards. I have to admit this one caught me by surprise, and when I shared it with my singles Bible study, the leader, a godly man still looking for a wife, looked troubled. Could it be his peers, single men who profess faith in Christ, are intimidated by the standards they hear preached from the pulpit? Standards written about in popular books like *Wild at Heart* and *The Sacred Romance?* But as you read the responses of the men in my survey, you become aware that they mean every word of it.

"Christian women are just plain too picky, especially about finding a man who's spiritual enough," wrote one man. "If they find themselves being pursued by a guy they genuinely think is a believer, whom they find reasonably attractive, and who they think would make a decent husband, they should just marry him. Instead, all the women who are still available seem to be holding out for some superspiritual guy who wants to be an overseas missionary in a Third World country, and whom they feel some kind of amazing 'click' or 'chemistry' with."

I find that I enjoy the company of non-Christian women far more than that of most Christian women. I just don't think they have bought into the popular tripe about what a man is supposed to be (thank you, Wild at Heart…Captivating*).*

In defense of my own gender, of the single Christian women I know, most have very realistic spiritual expectations of the men they date and hope to marry. Yes, they long to find someone who shares their faith, but they know that men are humans too, fallible creatures who mess up sometimes and need grace as much as we do. If anything, the women I know err on the side of giving too much latitude to men, sometimes blurring the lines between someone who says he believes in God (a nominal Christian) and a real believer. But that's not what showed up in the responses of the men who took my survey. Quite a few vented their frustration about the too-high standards of Christian women.

"Christian women have been fed a lot of misinformation about what actual men are like," writes one fed-up man, his frustration dripping from every line. "Reality check: there are no white knights or heroes out there. We can't rescue you. Sorry. And the 'Jesus is my boyfriend' thing is a little weird. I'm not saying you should lower your expectations. Rather, you need to readjust them, just as many men need to realize that actual women aren't like the airbrushed porn stars of their fantasies. I find that I enjoy the company of non-Christian women far more than that of most Christian women. I just don't think they've bought into the popular tripe about what a man is supposed to be (thank you, *Wild at Heart...Captivating*). Stop overlooking the men around you who don't have high paying/high prestige jobs. Real men are rough around the edges."

Just what does the book *Wild at Heart* (by John Eldredge) say about men? The book's marketing description on Amazon.com reads as follows:

> Helping men rediscover their masculine heart, this guide to understanding Christian manhood and Christian men offers a refreshing break from the chorus of voices urging men to be more responsible, reliable, dutiful...and dead. God designed men to be dangerous, says John Eldredge. Simply look at the dreams and desires written in the heart of every boy: To be a hero, to be a warrior, to live a life of adventure and risk. Sadly, most men abandon those dreams and desires—aided by a Christianity that feels like nothing more than pressure to be a "nice guy." It is no wonder that many men avoid church, and those who go are often passive and bored to death...Eldredge gives women a look inside the true heart of a man and gives men permission to be what God designed them to be—dangerous, passionate, alive, and free.

In reading through the responses of men throughout this survey, I heard plenty of passion and expectations, but also a world-weariness. Some seemed even more jaded than women about the state of single Christian America.

"Christians put unrealistic expectations on each other," said one man in his early 30s, who answered that he would like to be married someday if he meets the right person. "There seems to be this feeling that because you're a Christian, you must be perfect or more normal than others. Fact is, we're all human and imperfect, so we need to accept that fact, or else we'll always be frustrated at being disappointed in our significant other."

Unrealistic expectations—and modern singles' propensity to have a checklist of requirements for their ideal mate—actually work against true love. If it looks like love, acts like love, and has the staying power of love, then it's probably the real deal.

"The dating scene is okay as far as it goes," writes another man. "It's the progressing-to-marriage scene that's a problem. I wish women didn't feel they need a light shining down from heaven on a man and a voice booming 'He's the one' in order to make a decision. My last girlfriend wouldn't marry me because she felt she wasn't getting a clear signal from God that I was 'the one.' It was incredibly frustrating, and her breaking up with me broke my heart."

Somewhere out there, I can't help but think there's a young woman who realized too late that true love was standing right in front of her, but she let it slip away.

Women who strike a gracious balance between accepting men as they are—admittedly "rough around the edges"—yet gently prod them to be their best might find a true knight after all, or at least a knight-in-the-making. We all would do well to learn this lesson about looking for the best in the man or woman right in front of us.

In *Unhooked Generation* in a chapter titled "Finding True Love," Jillian Straus tells the stories of several couples who seem to have found what we all yearn for: a love with staying power, a romance that stands the test of time. She writes, "The one theme that takes precedence over everything else in all the stories of true love that I heard—a theme that, again, is totally at odds with the culture of emotional consumerism around us—is that, when something is wrong in these people's relationships, they consider first what they themselves might be doing to cause the problem."[1]

She tells the story of Clark and Sophia, a couple so right for each other, so madly in love, other people gaze at them with envy. Yet in the early days of their romance, Sophia almost gave up on the relationship, thinking Clark wasn't her "type." Paralyzed by the fear of making a wrong choice and of ending up divorced, for a long time Sophia resisted how right Clark was for her. After talking with a professional counselor, Sophia realized that while she'd been waiting for Prince Charming, a real man had shown up instead. "Once I got over my fear, I looked at Clark through new eyes," Sophia told Straus. "Love doesn't choose you. You choose love. Someone doesn't just show up on your doorstep, whether it is Tom Cruise or Edward Norton or whomever your fantasy man is, and you fall in love. I truly thought when the perfect man showed up, I would just feel all those things. But we do it for ourselves. If you have your walls up—fear and skepticism—you just won't fall head over heels. No one can bring it out if you are not open to it. Once I learned that, everything changed."[2]

We do ourselves a favor—and open ourselves up to the possibility of true love—when we drop our defenses, shred our checklists, and start seeing people as God does, with all the potential they possess.

Listen to what these men have to say about expectations:

> "The unrealistic expectations created by much popular 'Christian' literature has contributed to a climate in which a real man just can't measure up."

> "Christian women have high standards combined with a bad notion of reality."

> "Lower your standards. I'm not the apostle Paul! If I don't look like an evangelical, smell like an evangelical, have unattainable character and charisma, spend all my free time at church, have all my issues settled, have all my prayers answered, know Scripture inside out, love children...good grief!"

> "Don't wait around for Mr. Perfect. Accept dates even if they're not ideal. You might be pleasantly surprised at the men you get to know if you'll give them more a chance. God doesn't

always send Isaac's servant to find you. Sometimes Isaac himself comes, and he doesn't fit the description you'd imagined Isaac would have."

"Get real. Don't expect perfection. We make mistakes, and if that turns you into a man-hating woman, then too bad. If you can't deal with mistakes in a dating relationship, there's little hope for a long-term relationship."

"TOO MANY WOMEN BYPASS NICE GUYS IN FAVOR OF 'BAD BOYS'"

(Fear of rejection)

And since you know you cannot see yourself,
so well as by reflection, I, your glass, will modestly discover
to yourself, that of yourself which you yet know not of.
WILLIAM SHAKESPEARE

Careless of [Marianne's] happiness, thinking only of my
own amusement, giving way to feelings which I had always
been too much in the habit of indulging, I endeavored,
by every means in my power, to make myself pleasing to her,
without any design of returning her affection.
WILLOUGHBY IN JANE AUSTEN, SENSE AND SENSIBILITY

Funny, isn't it, the parallels between what women think about men and what men think about women? Although their frustrations are often inverted parallels, similarities do exist. While women lament that men are only looking for "supermodels" with the heart and soul of a saint, men say that too many women bypass nice guys in favor of "bad boys."

As much as I hate to admit it, there's a lot of truth to this sentiment. There *is* something alluring about the mysterious, heartbreaking, head-turning bad boy, and probably every woman has fallen for this type of charmer at one time or another. Think Johnny Depp as the slurring, swaying, swashbuckling pirate Captain Jack Sparrow in *Pirates of the Caribbean.* Or James Dean (for those of an earlier generation). Even though we know they would make terrible mates, we're drawn into their net—until we get bitten. And herein lies the hope for every man who complains that "nice guys finish last" or that women only want to date bad boys.

By the time a woman has *dated* a few bad boys and felt the full brunt of heartache they leave in their wake, she's ready for a truly good man. It's unfair to paint every woman this way, because some have the good sense (and sensors) to look for solid, good-hearted men from the get-go. But my own experiences and conversations with women confirm the veracity of this second frustration men voiced about single women.

Dr. Cara Whedbee, a psychologist and the author of *The Point System: The Game Every Woman Plays—and Loses,* has done a lot of counseling with single men and women who wonder why in the world they can't find someone to marry. Whedbee told me that it's really a very common theme. When I asked her about the men who showed up for counseling, she described the kind of men this chapter focuses on: "I saw a lot of wanting in my one-on-one sessions with single men—they were single and wanted to find a woman. They weren't the bad boys; they were the nice guys, but because they weren't exciting, the women would go out with the bad boys. These nice guys were the ones the women should have been marrying, and the single guys I talked to harped on this."

The funny thing is, most women end up married to nice guys versus bad boys, so in a very real sense, nice guys finish first rather than last. By their very definition, bad boys are usually the ones who want to play the field, prolong the candy-shop mentality, have exacting standards for the women they date, and keep women dangling on a hook. While some of these exciting bad boys eventually turn into good guys (once they grow weary of the shallow dating game), most women are better off looking for a lump of coal with promise—the proverbial diamond in the rough—rather than choosing a man who just *knows* he's got it going on. How can he see past his own importance to love her more than he loves himself?

For the women reading this book, I offer this "note to self": *Forget bad boys! No matter how good-looking or charming they are, they will only break my heart in the end.*

And for the men reading this book who fall into the good-but-overlooked category, take heart: some worthy woman out there who's tired of being treated badly will see you through lenses she never bothered to put on before and spot a prize.

Here are the responses other men gave on this topic:

"Too many Christian women bypass nice guys in favor of 'bad boys.' Too many Christian women who've been burned before fail to deal with their woundedness and therefore aren't capable of developing healthy relationships with Christian men."

Some of the reasons I've been turned down for dates haven't made sense. Give us nice guys a reasonable chance, and you'll find out we can be suitable marriage partners.

"Women say they want one kind of guy but date another. The men who have grown up aren't out chasing women. Problem is, women still wish to be chased. The men who are chasing them are still immature, so that's who they date. The guy still chasing women is like a teenager. Why? Because the women out there still go for the bad boy, and that's why nice guys finish last. They say they want a nice guy but date the bad boy. 'Cause he's fun (at first). Their loss."

"Give us guys a chance and go out with us once in a while. One date doesn't equal marriage!"

"Some of the reasons I've been turned down for dates haven't made sense. Give us nice guys a reasonable chance, and you'll find out we can be suitable marriage partners."

"I especially hate it when I make an effort to be seen or recognized and no one notices. I would love to see someone interested in me. What am I doing wrong?"

"I don't know that I'm really frustrated. One must learn to be content in any circumstance. Though I have often observed that the woman I go after (and I do ask women out) will usually not be seriously interested in me. The woman who is interested in me is usually someone I'm not interested in, though I try to be open-minded if she is a Christian. My mother and my sisters tell me that most women are intimidated by my intelligence. Here is something I used to find frustrating; now I'm just used to it: When I ask a lady out on a date, if she isn't interested, the only honorable reply is to decline rather than make up some lame excuse. This seems to be a situation where otherwise godly women feel that lying is appropriate behavior. Men pretty much across the board lament this and have praises for the women who say no or that they aren't interested. Personally I always feel like I asked the right woman when she honorably declines my overtures."

"It's bad to be rejected."

"I think too many women have come to expect a perfect man. Too much demand for the exciting, confident guys, and not enough willingness to give quieter guys a chance."

"CHRISTIAN WOMEN DON'T KEEP THEM- SELVES ATTRACTIVE ENOUGH, AND MANY ARE OVERWEIGHT"

(A lot of Christian women are overweight or dowdy)

Love sees not with the eyes but with the mind,
Therefore is winged cupid painted blind.
WILLIAM SHAKESPEARE

Here we come to a tough topic. Christian men had quite a bit to say about the number of single Christian women who are either overweight or otherwise unattractive—and don't seem to think they need to do anything about it. This sticky issue is so important to men, and they're so wired to be visually stimulated, that a single woman ignores this reality to her peril. In cultures past, where men weren't bombarded by visual images of attractive females everywhere they turned, the standard for female beauty included a wider range of natural comeliness and, some might say, more realistic measuring sticks.

Of course, women have always endured beauty treatments and uncomfortable contraptions to make themselves more beautiful for the men of their day and time (think of the corset, foot binding, tattooing, plucking, piercing, stiletto heels, starvation diets, etc.). Our culture is no different. To a very real degree, the cultural standards of beauty impact all of us, and men respond to those standards of female loveliness when they see them.

"The truth these single Christian ladies aren't willing to accept is that if men found them more attractive, they would get asked out," wrote one man. "I believe, having spoken to many single women, that they want to blame their lack of attention from males on 'waiting on God's timing' or on men being too passive. But the real answer is that if women made themselves more appealing, then they really would get asked out more often. Looks do matter. Many Christians believe that looks shouldn't matter, but they most certainly do. The good news is that guys are hardwired to respond to a woman's attractiveness."

In her book *For Women Only: What You Need to Know About the Inner Lives of Men*, Shaunti Feldhahn opens her chapter titled "The Truth About the Way You Look" with these red-hot words: "WARNING! *Before you read any further, pray first!*...This chapter is about something our men desperately want us to know, but feel absolutely unable to tell us...The effort you put into your appearance is extremely high on his priority list." Feldhahn goes on to describe a time when a male colleague approached her after a focus-group session she led to gather live research for her book.

> "There's something I need to mention to you," Ted said, looking uncomfortable. "I think women have a blind spot in an area that they really need to understand." Taking a deep breath, he spilled the beans. "I don't think women know how important it is to take care of themselves and not to look like a slouch around their husbands."
>
> "You mean, not to be overweight...?" I ventured.
>
> "That's part of it, but that's not really it," Ted continued intently. "It doesn't mean you have to be a size 3. The biggest issue is that your husband sees that you are putting forth the effort to take care of yourself, for him. See, my

wife is 115 pounds, but her weight isn't really the issue. It's not about being tiny. If she doesn't take care of herself, dresses sloppily around me all the time, never exercises, and has no energy to go out and do things together, I feel like she's choosing *not* to do something that she should know is important to me. And then it becomes a real issue because it affects her ability to do things and her self-worth and desire—and then it affects me."[1]

Feldhahn wrote her book for married women (she has a companion title for men), so her readers are dealing with the realities that set in after a couple gets too comfortable with each other. Everyone knows it's easy to let yourself go after marriage, but if women (and men) value their relationship, they won't do it. Now imagine how much more pressure is on women to stay attractive and height/weight proportionate *before* we find a mate!

The men who wrote in about this topic were blunt, protected by anonymity. One said, "The biggest complaint most Christian men have is that many single Christian women are overweight or don't have much sex appeal, etc…Ninety percent of the guys are interested in 10 percent of the girls in most churches because of this. Men are very visual. That's how we're wired. The problem is that we're in a society where sex appeal is more valued than ever before. Most single women outside the church, whom we see every day in public, have sex appeal and are going to the gym and are wearing stylish and sexy clothes. They are noticed by all the Christian men. It seems like many church girls buy their clothes from Wal-Mart, rarely go to the gym, and aren't as concerned about their looks. If we were in Iowa, it probably wouldn't be an issue. However, Orlando has pretty girls everywhere you go. *Guys don't want to settle for less than what they see every day!*"

The same man ends apologetically, yet honestly, "I know this seems shallow and a bit brutal, but it's what most Christian men complain about among one another."

Based on his market research, John Molloy considers a woman's appearance so important a factor in determining her likelihood of getting married that he lists it as one of only six guidelines, or statistical truths, for women who "wish to marry": *Keep in shape, watch your weight, and take care of your appearance.*

Specifically, he writes, "Women who are slender have an easier time meeting men and better odds of getting married...We found there was a marked difference between women who married and women who didn't in the way they cared for themselves...I am firmly convinced...that if a fairly attractive woman puts real effort into looking her best, she is more likely to attract men than a woman who is slightly better looking but doesn't put that same effort into keeping up her appearance."[2]

Only a handful of men remarked on this need for a woman to keep herself attractive, yet their words were so forceful, they warranted ink. To the women reading this book, I offer a heartfelt plea to take an honest look at yourself in the mirror and make the necessary changes. Even a start in the right direction will reap rewards, as Molloy attests in his book.

Consider this man's frank reply:

> I think when it comes to ladies not getting asked out, there is a lot of anger on the part of women toward men as a group. Lest you think you aren't attractive to men, just remember that Satan would love for you to believe the lie that nobody finds you appealing. Quite the opposite. But sometimes Christian women, especially, dress down because they don't at all wish to be a part of the worldliness of looking attractive. Big mistake. Before you get offended at this frankness, please hear me out, because there's both a bit of truth and a bit of hope here. I think the hard truth is that the really good looking ones do get asked out, and often. They're usually married (and sometimes divorced) by 30. I think it's very important for Christian women

not to blame their lack of response on the men but rather do something about their own physical appearance. Believe me, there's a lot that can be done that most single Christian women aren't doing. Now with that said, there's the other side of the road, and that's to fall into the trap of materialism and false perfection that women feel forced into. Nobody is perfect, and the image of perfection is virtually impossible to live up to.

"We Have a Very Real Fear of Divorce"

(The statistics are just too scary)

These violent delights have violent ends
And in their triumph die, like fire and powder,
Which, as they kiss, consume.

WILLIAM SHAKESPEARE, ROMEO AND JULIET

Not one woman in the survey mentioned fear of divorce as a worry or frustration in the world of romance, but a handful of men did, and their responses show just how deep the concern can run.

"I think many men such as myself have become somewhat gun-shy about diving back into the dating scene, *especially* if they've been hurt by an ex-wife's behavior, lack of trust, mental or emotional cruelty, etc.," wrote one man. "It takes time to heal these wounds, so this may explain why many men are a bit standoffish for a while—especially if they've been 'burned' as I was."

"Getting married these days is a very risky proposition for a man," another guy wrote. "It's incredibly scary. Add to that the fear of rejection when asking someone out, and it gets very close to being a 'Why bother? The return just isn't good enough' issue." The same man probably spoke for many when he added, "But still we seek. One thing that a woman can do is be more honest with us. Men know that 'I just want to be friends' really means 'I wouldn't date you if you were the last man on earth, and if you dropped dead, I would never miss you,' so why lie to us? Be honest with us."

The statistics are indeed scary, and maybe men's more pragmatic, analytical nature leads them to fear and reject the institution as a whole more than women. According the 2006 National Marriage Project:

> The increase in divorce…probably has elicited more concern and discussion than any other family-related trend in the United States…Although a majority of divorced persons eventually remarry, the growth of divorce has led to a steep increase in the percentage of all adults who are currently divorced. This percentage, which was only 1.8 percent for males and 2.6 percent for females in 1960, quadrupled by the year 2000. The percentage of divorced is higher for females than for males primarily because divorced men are more likely to remarry than divorced women. Also, among those who do remarry, men generally do so sooner than women.

> Overall, the chances remain very high—estimated between 40 and 50 percent—that a first marriage started in recent years will end in either divorce or separation before one partner dies…

> [However,] it should be realized that the "close to 50 percent" divorce rate refers to the percentage of marriages entered into during a particular year that are projected to end in divorce or separation before one spouse dies. Such projections assume that the divorce and death rates occurring that year will continue indefinitely into the future—an assumption that is useful more as an indicator of the instability of marriages in

the recent past than as a predictor of future events. In fact, the divorce rate has been dropping, slowly, since reaching a peak around 1980, and the rate could be lower (or higher) in the future than it is today.[1]

A woman who falls for a divorced man—especially one newly divorced—will find a wounded soul who needs forthright and loving interaction, even kid-glove treatment while his heart is healing. Both women and men emerge from divorces scarred, it's true, but our court system's tendency to favor women and punish men leaves many men stripped bare not only emotionally but financially as well. "If the lady isn't firmly Christian and determined to honor her vows ('Until death do us part'), then you can find yourself happily married, with kids, and wealthy one day, and divorced, childless, and a pauper the next, just because she 'didn't love you anymore,'" writes the same man quoted at the beginning of this chapter.

His fears are not unfounded. One man who took part in the survey cited "the prevalence of divorce" as the primary reason for the current marriage crisis in the church: "I've seen two male friends go through it (initiated by the wives) and can say that it sucks. That exposure makes me think twice about getting married until I'm 100 percent sure she's the one. It'll probably delay when I finally find someone, but it's not worth the risk—financially or emotionally."

Another man admitted honestly, "I'm not so sure I want to get married. My problem is the divorce rate: Fifty percent of all marriages end in divorce. Probably 25 percent of the others are not happy marriages."

John Molloy devotes a chapter of his book *Why Men Marry Some Women and Not Others* to the topic of marrying divorced and widowed men, and he gives the disclaimer: "Handle with care." He writes,

> With America's very high divorce rate, a substantial percentage of women who get married will wed a man who has been married before. While on the surface the

relationships that lead to these marriages seem to follow familiar paths, they are actually very different. The primary reason for these differences is that men who have been married usually come to a new relationship with financial obligations, emotional baggage, or children. Any one of these, and certainly various combinations of the three, will modify the nature of most relationships.[2]

Some of the men who mentioned divorce as a potential relationship hazard had been married before; others were sideline observers who didn't want to walk the same path that had devastated many of their male friends. For that reason, some of them put off marriage indefinitely.

For the grown-up children of the divorce culture—today's single men and women—"divorce was on every corner, every block, in every classroom," writes Jillian Straus in *Unhooked Generation*. "It is hard for us to even imagine a time when marriage truly meant 'till death do us part'...Even if you are from a happy home, chances are, many of the people you grew up with or date aren't. Widespread divorce has put a permanent dent in the idea of 'happily ever after' and created a generation of men and women highly skeptical of marriage."[3]

Yet once again, I have to stress the astounding fact that not *one* woman of the 86 female survey respondents cited fear of divorce as a hindrance to marriage in today's Christian dating culture. But several in the much smaller grouping of male respondents did chime in on this concern. For some, it's the only reason they're still single and may continue to be.

"christian women are too shallow and self-absorbed or just want to be 'friends'"

(Women are too self-absorbed • When we do ask them out,
they put up a wall: "I just want to be friends")

*Love is the most beautiful of dreams
and the worst of nightmares.*

WILLIAM SHAKESPEARE

Women confuse and frustrate men—that much is clear from the survey responses of men who voiced the complaint that single Christian women are shallow or so self-absorbed, they're a turnoff. One man said that women are "hopelessly stuck in the *Sex and the City* mentality that is pervasive in 21st century culture." This is a description of what that means in the real world: "Most women want to play around, flake out, remain uncommitted until their biological clock starts screaming. At this point, they feel they immediately deserve a wonderful man at the moment they demand such."

On the flip side of this sentiment is another equally frustrating one: that women often just want to be "friends." "At times you can't even be nice to a sister without the wall going up that 'We are *just* friends' or 'I'm not interested, so I'll keep this conversation short,'" laments another man. "Most of the times I'm truly being nice. It's the women who don't put up the wall that I respect the most and could get attracted to."

For many of the guys who complained about this female tendency, the opposite problem also occurs more than it should: "Also, you do go out, do call and thank them, and then need to explain what's going on."

Several guys wrote on this topic, genuinely wondering why women seem to want to be pursued, yet repel eager suitors at the same time. You can hear the disappointment in their replies. "There's no shortage of Christian women I do desire," writes one man. "I'm hung up neither with youth nor the physical, though it has some importance. The women I desire typically are only interested in a platonic relationship (which I'm okay with)."

Another man likened Christian dating to "being back in high school again or living in a small town. Everyone knows everyone, and people tend to gossip." Because of this, he feels he can only date someone who is a sure bet. "If we aren't compatible and I date someone else after, then I'm labeled as a player with all the girls," he says. "If you do get a girl's number, all the other girls seem to know immediately. Kind of a catch-22. I might be interested in a woman who ends up liking someone else."

The same man pointed out that Christian activities designed to bring people together "aren't always the most conducive way to break the ice or get to know someone. Often the activities can come off a bit cheesy. I feel like I have to walk on eggshells with Christians who don't know how to be real. I guess they're concerned about how others perceive them, and the gossip that could result if they don't act goody-goody."

Women want to do their own thing for years,
then as they approach the last of their child-
bearing years, they get serious, or rather desperate,

about having a family. Why can't this seriousness about
having a family happen when they're younger?

A male friend from my singles Bible study voiced the same concern about so many Christian women just wanting to be friends, and the mere mention of this trend—women either wanting to be "just friends" or clamoring to know where they stand with a guy after one date—brought shudders to the rest of the males in the group. Several male survey respondents weighed in:

"Women I meet from all walks of life—in church, in sports, in social groups, wherever—are ridiculous. They are self-serving, never do what they say, never follow through on a commitment, don't reciprocate contact, or never show a return of interest. Even common courtesy seems to be completely absent. On the flip side, if a woman is interested, she never conveys that information. I don't know if I speak for all men, but I grow tired of being the initiator and aggressor, only to be turned down. It would be nice for a woman to show some interest once in a while."

"Christian girls today are too confusing and are too self-involved. They're so involved with themselves that they don't care about the people around them. But I'm not talking about every Christian girl. Someone is out there for me. Ah, it's taking too long to find someone like that so I'll just find a non-Christian and convert her (laugh out loud)."

"I think the responsibility lies with both sides; career, fun, and success appear to be the main driving forces these days."

"Women want to do their own thing for years, then as they approach the last of their child-bearing years, they get serious, or

rather desperate, about having a family. Why can't this seriousness about having a family happen when they're younger?"

"Women contribute to the problem by not making their availability known, not being what they say they are, and caring too
much about a man's education, age, or money."

"Blaming men is not the answer!"

"Women are proud and blame others rather than taking
responsibility."

19

"IT'S Hard to Tell christian women from Non-christians these Days"

(Some women claim to be godly but lead worldly lives)

If passion drives you, let reason hold the reins.
BENJAMIN FRANKLIN

To some men, Christian women seem to behave the same way non-Christian women do these days. "It's getting increasingly harder to tell the difference between Christians and non-Christians," writes one man. "I find many who say they're Christians but do things like sleep around, have live-in boyfriends, drink to get drunk, smoke, curse, listen to all secular music, etc."

Another man writes that church has become so out of balance, he can't see the difference between a feminist and a female Christian.

Several women voiced this same concern about the opposite sex—that so-called Christian men push boundaries and expect sex from them—but in comparison to the number of responses on the other survey topics the sex issue for women garnered a much smaller share of the pie.

I'll never know whether the higher number of survey responses from men on this issue means that more Christian women are "living like non-Christians" nowadays or whether the prevalence of worldly Christian women just makes it seem like critical mass (compared to the "good old days") from the guys' viewpoint. I do know this: the majority of women who took my survey claimed to be virgins, and quite a few men did as well. When I told a friend about this finding, she snorted: "People lie through their teeth, even when it's anonymous." But I'm forced to take the results at face value and conclude that, at least among the women in my survey, chastity wins out over immorality.

Champions for Marriage

The pressures of the culture we live in weigh heavily on us all, and rare is the single man or woman who is immune to temptation of any kind. Especially among the divorced—who know what it's like to be in a long-term, intimate relationship—going from regular sex to no sex can be as jolting as an electric shock. But psychologist Cara Whedbee believes that churches have to keep preaching the purity message and become wholehearted advocates for marriage. Because we live in a society that values casual sex and "disses" marriage, even Christian singles get caught in the current.

"Because marriage is no longer valued, people won't set others up and encourage commitments. That sentiment is just no longer there," says Whedbee. "We're so against marriage now, and so in favor of living together. Or if you do get married, it's almost like dating—hey, if it doesn't work out we'll get divorced. You see it in the media, in movies—why get married? For those who do get married, a prenup is the big thing. But that just sends a nonverbal message that they don't think it's going to work out. Society is perpetuating the message that marriage isn't sacred anymore; marriage isn't necessary anymore. People don't buy into the biblical interpretation anymore. Not even subliminally. Instead, they overtly buy into the culture's live-together mind-set, even in the church."

Whedbee says it's become common at her church, where her husband works as a music minister, for the leadership to discover that young couples in ministry roles are living together. "And then somebody has to take them aside and say, 'Hey guys, this isn't right.' Especially the younger generation. They see it on TV and *have* seen it all their lives. Even at Christian schools, everybody sleeps together. You seem judgmental when you say there's a reason why you're not supposed to sleep around. You come across as too spiritual. It all starts with the youth culture. One study said that 85–90 percent of those who signed the True Love Waits petition had premarital sex."

Whedbee believes that men pressuring women to have sex is the mitigating factor, but there also exists a pressure among women—especially younger women—to live up to the culture's casual-sex creed.

If you find yourself struggling with sexual immorality, or any other "worldly pleasure" unbefitting for a Christian man or woman, seek out a confidant and ask that person to pray for you, that God will give you moral strength in times of sexual temptation. Truly, at some point in our single journeys, we may all face such temptation, but the choice of action is still ours. Remember the words of the apostle Paul, who kept such loving watch over the young church at Corinth, still fresh from the world:

> Flee sexual immorality. Every sin that a man does is outside the body, but he who commits sexual immorality sins against his own body. Or do you not know that your body is the temple of the Holy Spirit who is in you, whom you have from God, and you are not your own? For you were bought at a price; therefore glorify God in your body and in your spirit, which are God's (1 Corinthians 6:18-20).

20

"Christian Women Aren't Available"

(Where are these attractive single women you speak of...?)

If it is your time, love will track you down like a cruise missile.
LYNDA BARRY

Love sought is good, but given unsought is better.
WILLIAM SHAKESPEARE, TWELFTH NIGHT

The searching lover's lament—"Where *are* you?"—is perhaps as old as the second generation of humankind. And when we're in search mode, of course, the possibility of real and lasting love seems to elude us. Everywhere we turn we see *happy* couples, *married* couples, *engaged* couples. The guy or girl in the next cube over at work goes on and on about the wonderful person he or she met, and inwardly we groan—and wonder when it will be our turn.

It remains one of the biggest ironies of our day that we have more singles than at any other time in American history, yet the number-one complaint is that it's difficult to meet someone. Another irony: When you're caught in the grip of a singles slump and the years begin to tick by, the inability to meet someone seems to grow exponentially. And then the years *really* pile on.

Men have always seemed to have the upper hand in the availability market, regardless of what statistics say. But don't tell that to a guy who's looking for a wife with all the intensity of a wilderness scout. Says one man who responded to my survey, "I came from a church of around two hundred people with virtually no single women my age. I tried a larger church, and it seemed most everyone quickly disappears as soon as the service is over. Where are these attractive, eligible, single women you speak of?"

"I find it very frustrating that I encounter so few single women (Christian or not) of an appropriate age," wrote another man. "Too often, I only meet somebody in passing. Women seem to expect too much of a first date and don't seem open to the prospect of accepting a date with somebody they've just met. When I try to meet people online, I'm frequently annoyed by the number of women who ignore me when I try to introduce myself. If you aren't interested, it would be courteous to send a polite 'No thanks.'"

Following are a few more responses men gave regarding the scarcity of eligible single women:

> "It isn't so much what women have or haven't done; it's just that in my situation and social circles (including a very small church), I don't know any single Christian women who aren't dating anyone, and I think many Christians are in the same boat. We won't go to a club to meet people, and if you live in a small town and attend a small church, there is very little opportunity to meet people."

*Where are you? Send a SASE, picture,
and résumé to my address.*

"Eligible single women live thousands of miles away (laugh out loud)."

Where are you? Send a SASE, picture, and résumé to my address. (Joking of course. You don't have to include the SASE.)"

"Where are you hiding?"

PART 4

WHERE DO WE GO FROM HERE?

THE FIELDS ARE WHITE UNTO HARVEST—IF YOU KNOW WHAT TO LOOK FOR

It's hard for Christian men and women to take God out of the marriage equation, and we wouldn't even want to. At the same time, the cultural realities we live with force us to do more than simply drift with the tide; that is, if we're serious about finding a mate. The good news is that even in these marriage-unfriendly times, the fields are "white unto harvest" if you know what to look for.

When a woman decides she's ready for marriage, she sends out a different "vibe," and men can almost always pick up on it. That vibe usually comes across in one of two ways: as a calm, collected readiness to move into the next phase of womanhood (marriage) or as raw desperation. The first vibe is actually very attractive to a man, or at least to a man who is looking for a wife. But men can sniff out a truly desperate woman a mile away, and most of them run from her. If you think you're sending out desperate vibes, take a step back and assess what you're doing right and wrong. Ask God to replace your *desperateness* with *readiness,* and remember that all it takes is meeting one good man. A single day and a chance meeting really can change the course of your life.

The Great Divide

Dr. Cara Whedbee, the psychologist mentioned earlier, relates the story of one young woman who had what she calls a "stigma" on her. "She couldn't find anyone to marry, and that was part of the problem—it's the desperate vibe, and men can smell it. It's almost like the fear vibe that dogs can smell. You ask any man, and he'll tell you about it: 'She was wanting to get married, and I just wanted to date.'"

Whedbee admits that it's easy to tell someone, "Don't focus on getting married; focus on your life instead," but it can be really hard to live it out. (Though she's happily married, she can sympathize.)

She's not the only one who tries to help desperate singles integrate more naturally into the singles culture. Singles pastor Brad Goad notes a discernible lack of desperation in the singles he would classify as healthy, but that still leaves plenty who are desperate. And with a majority of divorced singles in his group (60–70 percent), there's plenty of baggage in the mix.

Goad talks compassionately about the singles he ministers to every week. And like any shepherd, he has a trained eye that detects crucial differences among his flock. "If we just deal with the 35-and-older group, about 50 percent have never been married, and of those singles, I see two main categories: those who are very career driven (male and female), and those who are, for lack of a better word, social misfits. They don't have the skills that would help them connect with people in a social setting. The first category of singles are very sharp and skilled, and they're also very active in church. It's not that they don't want to get married, but their lives are kind of on a roll. They're confident in who they are in Christ and what they bring to society as well as to the church, and they don't feel inferior or incomplete. I know that some of them want to be married, but they're not desperate. If there's a connection with someone, then great."

The other group, he admits, is "definitely wanting to be married, maybe out of sheer loneliness." In his ministry, Goad often meets one-on-one with the singles who fall in the latter category. He describes meeting with one divorced man in his 50s who longs to remarry but whose life isn't adequately prepared for a wife. The man isn't financially stable enough to be married, he's overweight and unkempt, and he lives in a one-bedroom apartment. But like anyone with a true pastor's heart, Goad holds out hope. "He's come to an awareness that he needs to make changes," he says. "He realizes he's not ready to be involved in a healthy relationship."

Goad says he believes Christian singles groups will always have a tension between those who are desperate to get married and those who are satisfied with life as it is. The irony, he admits, is that the first group's frustrations will likely grow because they haven't prepared themselves emotionally, spiritually, or physically to have a spouse. Meanwhile, "those who are ready but don't get married are probably going to increase in number. They go out some, but their social needs are met. They have a contentment about them."

Unfortunately, among the six hundred singles Goad ministers to, the women are more mature overall than the men. "Those guys in their late 30s and early 40s who are successful, if they've made it that long without getting married, aren't as eager to go out and get into a relationship that might lead to marriage," he states, validating John Molloy's findings.

However, even those men and women who need to work on themselves before seeking a mate will someday, in all likelihood, find a husband or wife. The good news is that most of us do! Until then, there are some specific ways to go about your search for a mate.

Strategic Thinking

Once you sense the time is right, start being intentional about putting yourself in places, and with people, that will nudge you in the direction of marriage. This might sound overly simplistic—even contradictory to what I just said about avoiding the desperation vibe—but once you have tools in place, you won't feel like you're floundering in deep water. The right approach—a combination of faith in God and purposeful thinking and action—will likely turn the helm of your ship into new waters that contain the very real possibility of marriage.

But wait, you might be thinking, *what about all those scary statistics that say there aren't enough single men to go around?*

Newsweek's infamous article "The Marriage Crunch," based on a study by Harvard and Yale, caused a firestorm of panic in 1986 when it proclaimed that women over 40 are "more likely to be killed by a terrorist" than find a husband. Later studies and articles encouraged women telling them it's "Not Too Late to Meet Prince Charming After All."[1] But for many single women, the damage was already done. Fear thrummed in their subconscious minds like an engine that won't shut off.

As years went by, the statistics only seemed to get worse, and for Christian women, the gap between available men and women appeared to be a virtual chasm—particularly after prolific singles writers cited a Barna Research finding that there are 11–13 million *more* single Christian women than there are single Christian men. But are the scary statistics true? Do they hold up under scrutiny? Candice Watters of *Boundless* decided to find out. In her article "Plenty of Men to Go Around," she opened with a scene that prompted her to write about the topic in the first place:

> "I think I may have raised my daughter to be lonely." That's what a friend of mine said during our conversation about the seeming famine of eligible Christian men. We were seated around a huge oak dining table, eating dinner with six single women and talking about the challenges they face in our culture.
>
> Included in the conversation—seated directly opposite my friend—was her daughter. I tried to gauge her expression following her mom's pronouncement. *How does she maintain faith in the face of such doubt?* I wondered. She's a beautiful 22-year-old with long dark hair

and blue eyes. Surely the other girls around the table felt in her shadow, *If she's not likely to marry, what hope is there for me?*

...A few weeks after the dinner I was talking to another friend who was writing an article about the challenges single women face. She was trying to respond to the charge that because there are so many more Christian women than men...maybe we should set aside the prohibition against marrying nonbelievers in favor of the Genesis creation mandate to marry and be fruitful and multiply. "Given the lack of men," she asked, "should we be encouraging single women to simply find a nice, moral, but unsaved man to marry?"[2]

Frustrated by the sheer shock value of the Barna statistic, Watters went digging. When she checked Barna's Web site, she read that as of the year 2000, "the survey data show that nearly half of the nation's women have beliefs which classify them as born again (46 percent), compared to just about one-third of men (36 percent). In other words, *there are between 11 million and 13 million more born again women than there are born again men in the country.*"[3]

Watters quickly realized that Barna was talking about *all* Christian men and women, not just the single ones. The second critical factor she noted was that the statistic was outdated by as much as six years! The good news, she writes, is that "Barna's 2006 numbers show the gap is narrowing." And the news for singles is even better. Watters writes,

So what about Christians who have never married? The surprising reality is that there are more men than women—a lot more. The 2006 Statistical Abstract of the United States identified 29,561,000 never-married men compared to 23,655,000 never-married women—*that's almost 6 million more never-married men than women.*

If you apply Barna's most recent faith percentages to the totals for never-marrieds, you come up with 12,120,000 never-married Christian men for 11,590,000 never-married Christian women—a variance of 1,530,000 *more* Christian men…I feel like celebrating.[4]

Armed with statistical proof that the "There aren't enough men to go around" claim is a well-publicized fallacy, single Christian women can concentrate instead on preparing themselves to be the kind of women that good men will want by their side—for life. The pertinent question then becomes, So where are these single Christian men? The Barna Research study did reveal that more single women than single men are in church, but that doesn't mean you can't find a God-fearing man elsewhere.

Separating the Wheat from the Chaff

I'm not an expert at love and relationships, but rather a journalist by nature, so my assignment for this book has been to take the pulse of the single Christian landscape, report on the findings, and then ferret out the best wisdom and practical advice I could find on the topic. In this case, the advice is all about moving from singleness to marriage—and I'm talking directly to women here. It turns out that there are things you can do to find a prospective mate—or move a budding relationship forward—and it all starts with looking for the right kind of man: the marrying kind.

In his book *Why Men Marry Some Women and Not Others,* John Molloy notes that when he completed the initial market research for the manuscript, one of his better researchers, a woman named Beth, wanted to read the results. According to Molloy, her problem was that "men who are averse to commitment were drawn to her like bees to honey." After reading the report, Beth angrily dropped it back on Molloy's desk and called him a male chauvinist. After he recovered from shock, he asked her what made her think that.

"You reinforce the myth that the reason men don't commit is that the women in their lives do something wrong," she steamed. "That's nonsense. In most cases, it's the man in a relationship who decides he isn't ready or doesn't want to get married, and he makes this decision without any help from the woman. No matter what some women do, there are certain men who are never going to commit. Unless you recognize that, you've missed the whole point. If you want to do women a real service, help us identify those losers before we get involved with them."[5]

After apologizing to Beth, Molloy admitted she had a point. His interviews with single men *had* shown that there were men who wouldn't commit. He also realized the valuable service he could provide women by identifying those men who were worthy of their attention as potential mates—and those to weed out. Molloy came up with a eight helpful tips.

1. Look for a man who's ready to commit. Molloy found in his research that there's an age when a man is ready to marry, or what he calls the "age of commitment." The specific age varies from man to man, but discernible patterns emerge:

- Most men with a high-school diploma start thinking about marriage as "a real possibility" when they are 23 or 24 years old.

- Ninety percent of men who have graduated from college are ready for marriage between the ages of 26 and 33. "But this window of opportunity stays open *only for four to five years, and then the chances a man will marry start to decline,*" reports Molloy (emphasis added).

- Most male college graduates between the ages of 28 and 33 "are in their high-commitment years and likely to propose." This period of high commitment

for well-educated men lasts just over five years.
After 32, it starts to taper off, but they're still in a
high-commitment phase.

- Once a man hits 38, the chances he will ever marry
  drop dramatically. Chances that a man will marry
  for the *first time* diminish even more after 42 or 43.
  "At this point, many men become confirmed bachelors," writes Molloy.

- Once a man reaches 47 to 50 years of age without
  marrying, the chances he will ever do so drop dramatically.[6]

"One of the most common mistakes young women make is to
assume that because they're ready for marriage in their early- or
mid-twenties, the men they date are as well,"[7] writes Molloy. But his
research shows that is usually not the case. Instead, if a woman is serious about finding a mate, she should *date only men who have reached
the age of commitment.*

2. Look for a man who is tired of the singles scene. Molloy found
that the men who were most likely to consider marriage seriously had
not only reached the age of commitment, but they had tired of the
singles scene—the endless round of singles bars (for some), singles
events, group outings, casual dating, and parties filled with questing
singles. Instead, he and his researchers found that about a third of
newly married men said that six months to two years before they met
their brides-to-be, they weren't dating or going to singles hot spots as
often as they had been just a few years earlier. In the men's own words,
they were ready for "something else" or the "next step."

When the singles scene ceases to be as fun as it used to be, a man
is ripe for the real commitment of marriage. As you meet men, listen
for clues that they've reached this point in their lives. Watch their
actions too; they are the best barometer of a person's inner world. A

man weary of the round of singles activities is much closer to desiring one woman for life than his still-party-hearty brothers.

3. Look for men whose biological clocks are ticking. This may sound strange at first, but Molloy explains men have a biological clock too, and they're keenly aware that it's running down. His team of researchers spoke to 121 men in their 40s who were marrying for the first time. "Obviously, a man's biological clock isn't the same as a woman's, but men are often in just as much of a hurry to have children," writes Molloy. "They're not worried about physically being able to father a child, but about *being* a father to the child."[8]

A caveat: One of the main complaints single Christian women lobbed at single men is that they put off marrying so long that when they finally do get ready, they shop in the much younger market of available women. Why? The obvious reasons are not only because they can but because they want to become fathers, and a younger woman is the more likely candidate to provide that. These are the very points Molloy makes.

4. Look for a diamond in the rough. As the years go by and no serious suitors appear to claim you, it's easy as a single woman to despair and start to think, *What's wrong with me?* I heard this heart cry numerous times in the responses to my survey. What women sometimes forget is that many men feel exactly the same way.

Molloy and his team talked to dozens of men in their late 30s and early 40s who had given up on the idea of marrying. Most lacked one of three things: looks, height, or social skills.

"If I heard it once, I heard it a dozen times," writes Molloy. " 'If I could find a nice woman, I'd marry her tomorrow.' If you meet a man who has never been married and seems excessively shy, it doesn't mean he's not interested in you, particularly if he's in his late thirties or older and not socially gifted. If you signal your own interest, you may find a nice guy who would love to settle down."[9]

Rachel Greenwald, author of *Find a Husband After 35,* concurs and expounds on the idea in her chapter titled "Market Expansion: Cast a Wider Net." Simply put, casting a wider net means looking for a husband who may not be the type you've always imagined. According to Greenwald,

> Most women, when asked what type of man they are looking for, will rattle off a list of five, ten, or fifteen criteria...Throw out your criteria and forget your type. I admit this action doesn't come naturally. You've had many years of thinking about "your type." The details of this type may include both external traits (height, hair color, age, profession) and internal traits (attitudes, beliefs, behaviors)...When women repeatedly date men with the same negative internal traits (say, needy, selfish, and arrogant), it's no wonder their relationships don't work out again and again. If this describes you, *now* is the time to break out of this pattern. Let me be *very* clear that I am not telling you to "settle." But I am telling you to be flexible. Your future husband may stand five feet eight rather than six feet tall. He might not know how to ski. He may be twenty years older. And horrors, he may be allergic to your cat! But if he is a wonderful person and you could fall madly in love with him, should you really overlook him?[10]

Looking for a diamond in the rough means you start looking at the single Christian men in your sphere with a new eye—an eye open to possibilities. Averse to bald heads? Consider that in this day and age, the shaved-head look is *in,* so naturally bald men have a step up on the ladder. Insist on a skillful conversationalist? Try carrying the thread of the conversation the first few times until he's warmed up to your presence. Sometimes the quiet, shy types hide a wonderful dry wit that only those closest to them get to know.

It's not uncommon to hear happily married couples tell funny stories about how they met—she didn't even notice him at first; he annoyed her with his boisterous sense of humor; she blended in with the other girls at the singles function until someone casually mentioned a topic she loved, and she lit up, taking him with her. These little nuances are the stuff of true love, and we limit ourselves by adhering to a strict list of must-have qualities.

Greenwald is so insistent that women throw away their "Mr. Right" list of criteria that she requires it in her 15-step program for finding a husband. Instead, she coaches, "The next time someone asks you what kind of man you're looking for, spread the word and answer simply, 'Someone wonderful.'...See what happens when you respond with those two little words and let someone think outside your box."[11]

Another way of restating this point about mining diamonds in the rough is to "reassess your options," as Candice Watters puts it. She explains:

> A lot of women have good friends who are men. They describe them by saying, "Oh, we're just friends; we've never thought of dating; we're not romantic." Too often we overlook men in the "just friends" category because we're not "attracted" to them...Instead of asking who you're attracted to, start asking *Of my friends, who would be a godly husband, strong partner and good father?"* Looking at men this way, you might be surprised who you're attracted to![12]

I have to tell you, there's really something to this. In my own college-aged singles group (many moons ago), quite a few male/female fellowship-group leaders wound up getting married. Of course, they never intended for anything to happen. But in the course of working side by side to build a lively Bible study or busy social calendar, they bonded as friends first—and then fell in love.

There's a lot to be said for relationships that are grounded on friendship first. If you do make the leap to marriage, once the dry spells set in (as they always do), you'll have your genuine *liking* for the other person—your friendship—to fall back on.

One female survey respondent evidently agreed with this reasoning: "Why don't you ever just plain ask for a casual date when it's obvious you're interested? *And why in the world wouldn't a good friend be the perfect candidate for a wife?* I'm not sure being single constitutes a crisis! But men certainly seem to be stuck on a look or a type that is very limiting."

5. Steer clear of confirmed bachelors and players. Easier said than done, right? That's the first cynical thought that sprang into my mind as I typed that heading. But there *are* good men out there—the results of the survey for this book reveal just how many single Christian men long to find a wife and labor under similar (if flip-side-of-coin) frustrations. The crucial thing is to distinguish between the men who truly want wives and those who are confirmed bachelors or outright players.

The first category, the confirmed bachelor, is easy to spot, says John Molloy: He's so used to living alone that he will list the pleasures of the solo life—coming and going as he pleases, not answering to anyone—as reasons for not marrying. Still, Molloy dangles a bit of hope. "Thousands of former 'confirmed' bachelors get married each year, usually to women they've known for less than a year or whom they've been going with for many years."[13]

The player, or what Molloy calls a "stringer," is a more dangerous type of man. "If you're dating a man who has had one or more long-term relationships with other women and didn't marry them, there's a real possibility he's a stringer," he writes. "A stringer is a man who strings women along. He likes to have a woman...[and] often tells women up front that he never intends to marry, so if and when he decides he wants to cut out, she has no reason to complain."

If you think you may be dating a stringer, Molloy advises a strict protocol: "Establish a deadline. If he doesn't commit to you within six months, get rid of him."[14] Sounds a lot like Candice Watters's advice about pulling a Ruth, doesn't it? But any sane woman realizes that a little pressure will work on some men but may have the opposite effect on others. Either way, you'll have your answer.

6. Avoid the buddy syndrome. Every single woman I know is so familiar with this pattern that one glance at the heading tells it all—and we groan collectively, for we've all been there. "A few bad habits can sabotage a relationship," writes Candice Watters, "yet single women seem to miss this. Some hang out with a 'buddy,' content with mere friendship, never daring to require him to state his intentions."[15]

Evidently, the buddy syndrome is especially prevalent among Christian singles, and the women let me know of their dissatisfaction with it. "Stop hanging out with women and *ask a woman on a date!*" one woman wrote. Another responded, "Men, please don't be afraid to ask us out on a date. One date doesn't mean it's a serious relationship."

Another big mistake single women make, blunt as it sounds, is spending all their free time with the same group, even after they've determined that no one in the group is a potential marriage partner. This isn't to say you should abandon your friends, but be open to branching out to new activities, new group events. Encourage those within your circle to invite single Christian friends and co-workers they know from other venues—cross-pollinate. An ever-widening circle of acquaintances can only serve to help all of you meet someone new with possibilities.

Too many single women also get sloppy when it comes to the boundaries they set—or fail to set—in their lives. But this is an area worth serious attention. "If you want a mate who respects you, you have to respect yourself. That means setting high standards for your relationships," asserts Watters. "Are you the gal guys come to for advice about other women? Do you spend all of your time with a guy who's not your boyfriend? Are you an open book with a man who hasn't asked for a commitment? If you've answered yes to any of these, you may need better boundaries to protect your time and your heart."[16]

7. Keep your cards close (sexually speaking). Growing up in the South, I heard a common refrain: "Men don't buy a cow when they can get the milk for free." Of course, the meaning inherent in those words—which has nothing to do with cows and everything to do with sex—hasn't lost its potency over the decades (centuries?) since they were coined. In our free-for-all culture, Christian singles may find themselves struggling to stay sexually pure, but the women certainly have good reason to. In her article "Finding a Husband," Candice Watters writes, "If you're having sex outside of marriage, you're diminishing your sexual power and your ability to find a good match. Instead of enhancing your relationship, sex will dictate it, setting the agenda and biasing all of your decisions."

She points out that some women have premarital sex and then wonder why their partner has no momentum toward marriage. Instead, be the mysterious one, the woman who retains her sexual allure by keeping her purity intact. "Unmet sexual longing is a powerful motivator for men and women alike," contends Watters. Our grandparents seemed to understand this far better than we do, and as a result, they often had short courtships. "Men having their sexual needs met casually have fewer reasons to sign up for all the responsibilities of marriage," she writes.[17]

8. Ask your friends and relatives for help. No woman wants to advertise that she's available and seem like the pathetic unmarried cousin or aunt or sibling who "still hasn't found a man." Yet asking for help is exactly what you should do, according to the experts. Rachel Greenwald is brash about it, encouraging women to "spread the word" to all their friends, co-workers, and relatives that they are indeed looking for someone—"someone wonderful" (Greenwald's two-word criteria).

Candice Watters takes a more philosophical approach, stating that "until recently marriage enjoyed culture-wide support…Friends and relatives were willing partners in helping singles meet the eligible bachelors in their lives."[18] Her own mentor in the journey toward marriage—the professor's wife mentioned earlier—counseled her and the other girls in her dorm to be intentional about seeking marriage. "The culture we live in is anti-marriage," her mentor said. "So many of the customs and unwritten social rules that once helped bring young men and women together, now seem to pull them apart…We are in limbo without the structures and social supports. We don't even know if potential mates believe in marriage the same as we do. Just how courtship should be done is up for grabs. Not because it *should* be, but because it *is*."[19]

This mentor (Mary Morken) encouraged her young protégées to "stand in the gap for each other, facilitate the courtship process and through self-disclosure, express your beliefs about marriage and courtship within your group of friends. You never know, that group may include your future mate."

"Talk about marriage," Morken challenged the girls. "Don't be afraid of the subject. You are young, godly men and women, you should want to be married and be willing to do the work to get there."[20]

Watters adds that she and her friends were a little shocked at their mentor's bold stance, but they also knew they weren't having any success doing things their way.

In the end, writes Watters, "Mary's encouragement really came down to one word: intentionality. American women are known for high-achievement in every area but the one we say we value the most: relationships. Sadly, we're members of a generation which, on the whole, desires marriage, but doesn't know how to get there or believes there's no rush to make it happen."[21]

In my research for this book, I came across this powerful principle in action, and it was a story with a happy ending. A co-worker, Rene, told me that when she was in her early 30s and happily married, she had an unmarried girlfriend around the same age who was somewhat quiet in nature and worked in an office staffed mainly by women. "I realized one day that my friend Darlene was never going to meet a man on her own and needed some help," she told me. Excited about her new "Emma" (matchmaker) role, Rene enlisted the support of her husband. In typical male fashion, he rolled his eyes and told her to butt out of Darlene's love life. "Eventually the right man will come along. You'll see," he said. But Rene wasn't content to sit idly by.

A few months went by, and a man in his 30s got hired at the company where Rene's husband worked. This event in itself meant nothing to her husband, but Rene heard how glowingly he talked about the new hire—what a nice guy he was, how he was "back on the market" after a divorce, and so forth. The wheels started turning in her brain. She encouraged her husband to arrange a double-date dinner out, inviting his new colleague. She in turn would invite her friend Darlene. Her husband resisted at first but finally relented. And, as they say, the rest is history. The couple hit if off instantly and got married three months later. And now they're about to celebrate their eighteenth wedding anniversary.

Dealing with Rejection—the Downside of Dating

By its very nature, dating involves opening yourself up to casual rejection and the risk of unrequited love. For this reason alone, some people, most notably Joshua Harris, author of *I Kissed Dating Goodbye*, discourage dating and encourage Christian singles to get to know each other in emotionally safe group settings. Only when they mutually discern God putting their lives together in a permanent way should the man initiate a courtship phase. *Courtship* is defined as meaningful time spent together (dating) with a goal toward matrimony.

While I can't help but recognize the wisdom in Harris' approach, it seems to be less and less practical the further away from the nuclear family a single gets. In other words, men and women in their late 30s or mid-40s don't always *have* the large network of like-minded Christian friends that guys and girls in youth groups or college-age church groups do. By this time, your world is more insular, many (if not most) of your friends are already married, and you find yourself wanting to spend one-on-one time with potential mates anyway.

Of course, the wisdom of keeping things casual until you both discern that God is joining your lives still applies, but it's difficult to advise a 40-year-old man not to take a woman he's interested in out for dinner or coffee. After all, conversation is still the best way to get to know someone. If you happen to meet in a group setting, or through mutual friends, it makes sense to discover that person gradually in the same settings, but sooner or later you'll probably want to spend some time one-on-one so you can both see if there's a mutual connection. Hence, dating and the possibility of rejection either early in the game or sometime down the road.

Dating coach David Wygant, coauthor of *Always Talk to Strangers: Three Simple Steps to Finding the Love of Your Life,* wrote an article called the "7 Dating Ups and Downs." It offers the following advice for singles who tend to beat themselves up over the ups and downs of dating:

1. Stop the mental post-date recap abuse. You went out with somebody with whom you thought you had a connection, and it turns out you didn't. So now you're going to mentally torture yourself for the next four days trying to figure out what you said wrong…The post-date recap is a form of mental torture. You will never know what that other person is thinking unless they call you. If they don't call, it really does mean that he or she is just not that into you.

2. I texted them the next morning and said, "I had a great time last night," and they never texted back. So what? You had a great time last night. So did they. They just woke up, and their post-date recap was different from yours. They probably had a good time, but when they thought about it, the chemistry and the "it" factor wasn't there. It's not about you. At least you were honest. So you did all you can do.

3. Should I have said something different in my voicemail message? You left a voicemail message and now you're replaying it in your head a thousand times…When it comes to voicemail messages, the shorter the better. From an old sales technique, I always prefer to say, "Last night was fun. I have something really funny to share with you the next time we speak." That's it—it creates a little bit of intrigue, a little bit of mystery and no mental torture.

4. Stop giving your power away to one person. If a two-hour date can cause you to give away all your power and confidence, then you need to learn to embrace yourself and love yourself more. This is just one person you went out with for two hours. They don't know what an amazing person you are…Whether they choose to hang with you again isn't the issue. The issue is that one person does not determine your worthiness. If I go out with someone and I have a great time but they never want to see me again, I'm still a great person the next day.

5. In order to feel better about dating, you need to think abundance. Just because you think you like somebody and they don't call you back, this is not the last person in the world you're going to meet… Realize that if it doesn't work out with one person (or 10 people), there are plenty of other people out there who do want to hang out with a fantastic person like you.[22]

Online Dating: Do or Don't?

At some point in your singles sojourn, you'll most likely be tempted to give online dating a try. I sure did! (In case you missed them, see my horror stories in chapter 1.) Yet some people *do* meet the love of their lives on Internet dating sites. We've all seen the glowing testimonials, and they can be hard to resist. What makes it even harder is when a friend—or even a friend of a friend—has success with e-dating, gushing over how she met the wonderful man she eventually marries. As I stated earlier, however, I believe the cons to Internet dating outweigh the pros.

Seems I'm not alone. Psychologist Cara Whedbee flatly states that she wouldn't recommend e-dating sites, especially the ones that send you "matches" based on extensive personality tests. "What I've noticed about these sites is that the matches aren't the right person for you," she says. "The problem is they're matching you with a friend. You're getting all these compatible issues, but you don't get to see anybody else who's not your match. And we all know you've got to have that love factor. I have a lot of guy friends, but I'm not attracted to them physically, yet if I were single and dating online, the sites would probably match us together. The truth is, we're not a match at all. Whereas my husband and I probably wouldn't be matched at all. You need the love factor!"

A popular women's magazine carried a story that illustrates Whedbee's point in a powerful way and lines up with my own renewed conviction to leave love and romance to destiny rather than the Internet. The writer tells how, in her search for love, she created a profile and joined the hundreds of thousands of singles who have turned to the Internet for a shot at true love. After sifting through dozens of profiles and even meeting several men in person, she inevitably grew weary of the process, not to mention jaded in a way she wasn't before. All the men sounded wonderful in their profiles, but often that hoped-for spark just wasn't there when they finally met in person. Many guys the system considered a match for her proved to be anything but.

A little time passed, and the woman went to a party one night where she met an interesting man who caught her eye from across the room. As they started talking, he mentioned that he had tried the same online dating Web site she had. When he told her his screen name, she couldn't believe her ears. Here was a man whose profile she had seen many times—and passed over. He was actually much more attractive in person than he was in his photo, she discovered. And his engaging personality was the icing on the cake. From that chance meeting *in person,* rather than the static, impersonal medium of an online profile, a spark was lit and the two started dating.

You never know when love will enter your life or the face it will be framed in. It may result from a chance encounter at a video store or a blind date set up through a mutual friend. One thing is certain: When love finds us, we're never the same again. Love changes us from the inside out, and even unrequited love leaves its mark on our souls. As the poet Tennyson wrote, " 'Tis better to have loved and lost than never to have loved at all."

Of all the admonitions in this book, I want to end with the one I myself have found the most heartening: hope. For it is in hoping that we are our best and truest selves. And what better self could we offer to a prospective mate than one that "smiles at the future" (Proverbs 31:25 NASB).

Becoming a
Hopeful Romantic

A few years ago, someone said the words I most needed to hear as a single woman. Ironically, it was another single woman who uttered them—a bit of wisdom gleaned from her mother, I suspect. If I could tell her now, I would let my friend know how much her simple reply comforted my heart, and how many times it has anchored me when I despaired of ever finding "the one." They are words I want you to hear too.

Having just passed the time of year that privately makes every searching single wince—Valentine's Day—it was a relief when the words from this long-ago conversation floated back to me, as relevant as the day they were spoken.

My friend Heather had pulled me aside after our church's midweek worship-band rehearsal one night. The sparkle in her dark brown eyes reflected the joy of a newfound love in her life, a relationship that indeed turned out to be "the one" two years later.

"So how's everything going with Joe?" she asked, eager to hear the latest developments of my on-again-off-again relationship with a guy from church. I almost felt guilty when my disappointing answer stole the smile from her face. Things were definitely *not* so good, I told her, and it looked like Joe and I were headed for a dead end.

Before I could stop myself, I lapsed into that despairing mode all searching singles are familiar with. I call it the "Why has God forgotten me?" syndrome (you might also call it a pity party). When everyone around you seems to be coupled off or at long last meeting the man or woman of their dreams, you soldier on alone. You purchase your meals for one at the grocery store and wonder, *Has God forgotten my address?*

Sighing, I told Heather, "It's okay. I know God has someone special out there for me. I just wish I could find him."

She looked at me intently and shook her head. "No, Angie, he'll find you." My puzzled look must have told her the words needed repeating: *"The right man will find you."*

The words sank into my spirit as Heather continued. "Remember? The Bible says he who finds a wife finds a good thing…It's the man's job to find you. You just have to wait." She rambled on in this vein for a few minutes, but all my mind could register was an overwhelming sense of relief. The pressure was off; the search was over.

If you're a single guy reading these words right now, you may be thinking, *Great! So shove the burden onto our shoulders!* But believe me when I say this arrangement is *not* any woman's idea. Everything within us seems bent on trying to make things happen. We work ourselves into a frenzy trying to go here, be there, attend all the right functions, search online, and discreetly ask our friends for blind-date setups. But I have a hunch this isn't what God intended for our single-woman status to look like. In allowing men to be the hunters—the ones who do the searching and finding—He must have a perfect design up His sleeve.

Even though my friend's words comforted me the night I first heard them, the passage of time has a wearing-down effect. Sometimes the rest and peace inherent in those words get lost in the worry that time is running out. I find myself in search mode again, wondering about every interesting guy I meet, "Could he be the one?"

In her classic book *Passion and Purity,* Elisabeth Elliot talks about this rather unpopular notion of waiting, of being a single woman not intent on finding Mr. Right, but allowing God to bring him to you. The Bible is replete with examples of this pattern: When the time was right, God *brought* Eve to Adam; Abraham's servant went out and *found* a wife for Isaac; Jacob, traveling to a distant land, *found* the girl of his dreams in Rachel. But note this: All of them were going about the business of doing the work God had for them to do.

Not long ago I read a passage that brought Heather's words back to me. In the true story, a father asks his young teenage daughter if she ever worries about who she will marry and whether she is even interested in boys. The daughter laughs and says, "Oh, Daddy, you and I both know God has a special guy out there for me, and when the time comes He'll bring him along." Once again, those words of quiet assurance stopped me in my tracks. *Lord, give me faith like that young girl,* I thought.

We have no divine guarantee that a longing for something ensures ultimate satisfaction, but at least now I know (and keep reminding myself) that as a single woman, if God does have one special man waiting for me, it's not my job to find him. But that doesn't get me or any other single woman off the hook. We have a job to do as well; in fact, so does every single person looking to be a wife or a husband someday.

Cleaning House

It's ironic that in our culture we prepare for everything but marriage. We go away to college and study for four years to prepare for our chosen career. We may study for months before we take the SAT. A new driver in my state has to have a learner's permit for six months to one year before obtaining a driver's license. Participants in a theatrical production memorize lines and rehearse for months before opening night. First-time mothers and fathers have nine months to prepare for the big debut in their own lives, often going to parenting and Lamaze classes well in advance. Yet somehow we expect that everything will just fall into place where love and marriage is concerned.

Dr. Cara Whedbee has counseled many single people who ask, "Why can't I find a mate?" She told me that one of the biggest mistakes people make is rushing into relationships without getting themselves ready, or what I like to call housecleaning. Even Esther, the beautiful Jewess of biblical history who won the favor of a king and became queen of Persia, had to undergo 12 months of "beauty preparations" before she was presented to King Xerxes—or, symbolically, made ready for marriage (Esther 2:12). If we as singles take seriously the idea of entering marriage someday, whether for the first time or in a remarriage, we must also take seriously the process that will make us worthy lifelong companions.

Never-Marrieds: Don't Be a Jerry Maguire

When I asked Dr. Whedbee what she considers the most important advice for singles who want to prepare themselves for marriage, she reminded me that her answer would differ for never-married singles versus divorced singles wanting to marry again. "For someone who has never been married, you need to figure out who you are first and what you want," she said. "You do this so that when you finally get married, it's because you're a whole person—you're bringing two whole people together. You have to complete yourself; you can't be a Jerry Maguire, saying, 'You complete me.' Know who you are. Know what you like and don't like, what you need in a mate and what you definitely could do without. Know where you want to be in five years and how much older a potential mate you are willing to look at, because love can come from anywhere. Maybe you've exhausted all the possibilities in your community and are ready to move somewhere else. Mature whole people know who they are and what their purpose is in life."

This "knowing" may take time. Ask God to give you spiritual insight into the areas of your life that you've been blinded to up till now. Consider asking a trustworthy friend what are your best—and worst—traits. With that person's input, take an honest self-assessment. Are you a little too selfish? Too demanding? Do you still expect everyone to please you, or have you matured to the point where pleasing others brings you joy? "If you know who you are, and the person you're dating does not, then you're not on the same spiritual level, and he or she will know it right off the bat," says Whedbee. "If you do know all this and are still having issues, you're probably finding men or women who don't know who they are yet. My advice would be to go to different places, find a new hobby, maybe switch jobs. A good friend of mine started dancing lessons and met a guy there. You never know where love will find you. Mix it up, and you'll have a better chance of finding someone."

Divorced: Getting Over the Blame Game

For those who have lived through a divorce, Whedbee's advice takes a different—and perhaps more painful—tack. She recommends asking yourself the big question: "What went wrong?" Once you've honestly asked yourself that question, you must be willing to take ownership for your part in the failed marriage. "Even if you think it was all his fault, or all her fault, it still takes two to get married, and it takes two to make a divorce," says Whedbee. "It could be that you picked a wrong guy [or gal], or it could be that you choose cheaters. You need to figure out what caused the disconnect, what happened there. Then you need time to heal."

She recommends talking with a good Christian counselor who can help you untangle your knotted romantic past, point out destructive patterns in your life that you need to eradicate, and teach you coping skills. "I always tell people they need to develop that muscle, figure out what went wrong the first time, and fix it before they start looking for somebody else."

Most often it's wise to wait for a while before leaping back into the dating fray. The passage of a year or two will give you time to work through your issues, and you'll be in a better position to look for love again. When you do begin dating again, go easy at first, and get to know other singles as friends before leaping into love. Even if someone sweeps you off your feet, a good friendship foundation will put your relationship on solid footing.

For those divorced men and women who are also parents, Whedbee cautions against dragging your kids into the picture too soon:

> Once you feel ready to start looking around, you have to be really careful involving the people you date in your kids' lives. Kids are a lot more aware than parents think they are. Be open with them so you're not sneaking around or lying to them. Until you're really comfortable with someone and think he or she has marriage potential, don't introduce that person to your kids. That's the hardest part about dating again after you've been married.

Preach It!

What can we do as Christians to promote marriage in an antimarriage society? First, we have to "preach it," says Whedbee. We need to talk about why the Bible says to leave your father and mother and cleave to your mate (Genesis 2:24), why the Bible calls marriage sacred and a union between one man and one woman.

"Whenever my husband and I had issues we had to solve them ourselves," Whedbee says. "That's the only way to cleave. The problem is that many people never really leave their parents, so how then can they cleave?"

We can't shy away from the difficult topics—adultery, premarital sex, living together out of wedlock—just because our society says these are the new "norm." People are hungry for something different because what our society has offered them doesn't work, says Whedbee. "They're hungry, so preach it. Talk about it with other singles."

If you're in a position of leadership in a singles ministry, make sure it's a place where both men and women can feel comfortable—not a meat market. Women shouldn't feel like they're being ogled or that guys are hitting on them the first time they walk through the door.

And men shouldn't feel like they're being sized up as potential mates or smothered by desperate women. Help people be who God has called them to be.

Finally, bring the fun back to church. "Today people would rather go to a bar to seek excitement than to church," says Whedbee. "The fun place to be should be your church. Sponsor creative social functions like road trips and citywide dances. I've seen it work, with a lot of friends getting together from it. If that's your focus—to get together as friends and just have fun—then if something happens, it's icing on the cake."

In the Fullness of Time...

One of my favorite lines from a movie comes from *Romancing the Stone,* starring Michael Douglas and Kathleen Turner. In it, protagonist Joan Wilder, a romance novelist, talks to her literary agent on the phone about finishing her latest book. The emotion of the story has brought her to tears. Hearing her sobbing through the line, her agent teases her, calling Joan a hopeless romantic. "No," she counters, "not a hopeless romantic. I'm a hopeful romantic."

The first time I heard that line, it sank deep into my spirit, and somehow it has stayed with me through the years. It's like seeing the glass half empty or half full. Which are you? A hopeless romantic, frustrated by years of singleness stretching across the canvas of your life, or a hopeful romantic, living your life to the fullest, yet seasoning every day with a dose of expectation?

In the past year or two, God has brought one special phrase from Scripture into sharp focus in my life again and again. The phrase I'm talking about is that innocuous one we read in the more narrative parts of the Bible: "In the fullness of time..." I'm not a patient person. It's something I've struggled with my whole life, and so far, things haven't gotten much easier. But one thing God keeps doing to nudge me closer to *patient* is reminding me of His always-just-in-time calendar of events. I look back over the course of my life and marvel at how often something I prayed for, yearned for, waited for, and cried for finally came to fruition—but not a moment too soon. *Why did you take so long, God!* we lament, railing against the heavens like Scarlett O'Hara in the potato garden. But if we're honest, we'll probably recognize that God's actions in our lives, and the lives of those we love, occurred just in the nick of time. Just at the right time. *In the fullness of time.*

The phrase reminds me of an expectant mother. Happy to be pregnant, she grows weary by degrees as the months pass slowly, but always before her is the expectation of her baby—the culmination of her hopes in *the fullness of time.* In a similar way, we wait in hopeful expectation for God to place just the right person in our lives at just the right time. Maybe you aren't ready for a spouse at the moment. Perhaps you have quite a bit of housecleaning to do before God can bring a special man or woman into your life. But you can start praying and moving in that direction. Remember, a single day can change the entire course of your life. You may wake up tomorrow and see a face you've never seen before—and in that face you may meet a person who changes the course of your life. You may be closer to that "fullness of time" than you think!

Looking For Love Like a Peasant

So we're back to square one. Of all the responses generated by the singles survey, the most revealing was the one quoted at the beginning of this book. It bears repeating: Out of 120 singles, both men and women, not one said no to the question, "Do you want to be married someday?" To me this is remarkable—not to mention ironic—and made all the more so by our seeming inability to find marriage partners with ease. In the old days, a man could usually find a wife if he went looking, and a single woman could attract a husband by putting herself in socially acceptable places to be noticed. So what are we doing wrong? If the vast majority of single Christian men and women "want to be married someday," we're also right back to the question I posed to my Bible-study group: Why is it so hard to get married?

Aristocrats Versus Peasants

Jewish rabbi and relationship expert Shmuley Boteach, known as the "Love Prophet," believes he knows why singles today find it so hard to discover their soul mate. His theory is so sound and makes such sense in our confused world that I wish I had invented it. When it comes to love, Boteach writes, we've become a generation of "aristocrats" in search of the perfect match, when the real secret to lasting love—the attitude of a "peasant"—is available to us all along.

In his book *Dating Secrets of the Ten Commandments,* Shmuley Boteach writes,

> I often ask people, "Aren't you going to get married?" At that point I hear a strange response: "When I meet the right person." Sure, the idea is reasonable, but the sentiments are rarely so. Usually what I am hearing is a person telling me that they are waiting for a person to come along and impress them with their eligibility. This is the thinking of aristocrats, and leads nowhere. In dating, you should always be a peasant.[1]

To find the perfect soul mate, Boteach states, you should focus not on what you have, but on what you *lack.* We make one of "the biggest mistakes of all" when we go about finding a marriage partner by sitting down and making a list of everything we have to offer a relationship. Historically, this laundry list of qualities is the very thing the aristocracy took into consideration when making a match, whether it was the union of royals to ally two nations or the nuptials between the daughter and son of two land-owning families, for example.

In his work as a rabbi at Oxford University in London, Boteach noticed a curious phenomenon. He observed that the more successful a man or woman was, the more partners they dated, and the later they married in life. These men and women were so good at what they did for a living that they wanted to "hold out for the best."

For all our advancements in the modern world, Boteach writes, we've ignored the vast and all-important social changes that have swept the landscape. "Ours is a generation in which nearly everyone in the Western world is an aristocrat. Previous generations were not ones of empowerment. There was a small aristocratic class for whom everyone else worked and upon whom everyone was dependent. But while not everyone in the West today is wealthy, the vast majority are self-sufficient. We have our own jobs, own our own homes, can afford to take holidays and buy ourselves nice clothes. We can, thank God, employ other people to help us with the housework and nanny the children. We are the new class of nobility."[2]

This hard-won nobility has come at a price, however. With our self-sufficiency and consumer mind-set, we don't want to "settle" for any commodity, from our wireless plan to the neighborhood we live in. We strive for the best we can possibly attain. Sounds reasonable, you might say, but what that translates to in the romance department is most likely a lot of searching and a lot of disappointment. In contrast, the peasant class always knew they had a hard lot ahead of them, perhaps, but they tried to assuage that harsh reality by finding a good man or woman to love. Love was the one thing that might lift an otherwise dull, mundane life out of the murky waters of daily existence. A warm bed filled with a warm embrace at the end of the day would make it all worthwhile.

So while the peasant class "traditionally looked for one big thing in the person they dated," writes Boteach, "aristocrats have always looked for many small things. Because people with earning power—aristocrats—have greater choices about their lifestyle, they tend to make a laundry list of things that they would like to find in a relationship and marriage."[3]

Because aristocrats are so self-sufficient, not to mention confident, in what they bring to the table, they seldom seek to "share their lives with anyone." Instead, when they get lonely and decide to settle down, they look for a "partner." *Therefore, the very first move by the aristocrat who wants to find a companion is to take a look at themselves and list their attributes,* says Boteach.

The King of England wants to marry off his son. Well, he brings a kingdom to the table plus x amount of riches and x amount of noblemen who pay him homage and allegiance. He is then introduced to the daughter of the King of France. She also brings a kingdom, but does she bring the same amount of cash and prestige into the relationship as does the Prince? How many ladies-in-waiting are at her beck and call? Well, this will depend on the last battle her father fought and either won or lost. France's navy is currently weak while the Spanish Armada is strong. It's settled then, the Prince will marry an infant from Spain rather than a princess from France.

All of us are amused by the history of royal weddings over the past thousand years because they were all about business partnerships and political alliances and never about love and relationships. But I can't tell you how many people think this way today as well…

This logic is not flawed, for it is the thinking of aristocrats. But aristocrats can never be truly happy in love. At best, they can hope for a harmonious partnership. Those who wish to find a soul mate in their relationships are a completely different breed of person.

Indeed, they are the polar opposites of aristocrats. They are "peasants."[4]

The "needy, beautiful peasant" approaches the possibility of romance from the starting point of "What do I lack?" and looks for someone who can fill that need. A peasant's main asset on the Potential Soul Mate test is his or her vulnerability. Not having an overly inflated view of what they bring to the table, peasants date in order to find "a lifelong companion who will make them feel profoundly worthwhile, even if the rest of the world dismisses them as unimportant. Whereas the aristocrat dates and marries for many small things, the peasant dates and marries for one big thing: someone who takes away the pain and makes life a celebration. In choosing a soul mate rather than a partner, the peasant is given the greatest gift of all."[5]

Recapturing the Other Four-Letter Word

Shmuley Boteach has made a career out of helping people find lasting love, and for my part I'm glad to know there are individuals out there waving the marriage-is-worth-it banner. It makes all the frustration of waiting and searching worthwhile. Recently one of the guys in my singles Bible study announced that he's getting married for the first time, at age 45. He met the woman he's marrying online. The news made me smile, and I immediately thought, *One down, fourteen to go!* I hope someday we'll all be able to look back at our madcap single days and smile, remembering how interminable the in-between years seemed before we found the one man or woman who changed our lives. And I hope we never lose our sense of vulnerability or what Boteach calls "the four-letter word of relationships": *need.*

In his book *Why Can't I Fall in Love?* Boteach writes, "I frequently hear people telling their friends, 'The reason you don't fall in love is that you want love too badly...People can *smell* the need on you. Love won't find you until you stop looking for it.'" Then he poses the question, "Sound familiar? Looking for love has become something to be embarrassed about. You don't hear people talking about unemployment this way: 'I used to go to job interviews, looking to get hired by law firms. I found it absolutely humiliating, having to cozy up to the partners to get them to give me a job. So I decided I will never go for an interview again. I'll just live on the streets, with no money and no food. If some guy comes and offers me a job, I'll take it, but I will never search for it again.'"[6]

Need, the rabbi asserts, is the dirty little secret of dating that no one wants to admit. But when you're looking to fall in love, when you're looking for the happiness that comes from giving yourself fully to another, it's all about "opening yourself up, exposing your vulnerabilities, and creating a space where you and a lover can grow together." In short, Boteach says, it's about realizing that *need is good.* He concludes,

We all must remember, after all, that one of our goals in the search for romance is to find someone who needs us. Imagine how you would feel if your lover one day told you, "I love you, but I don't need you. I admire you, but I can live without you." The only way to find love is to embrace that sense of mutual need. If you truly want to fall in love—to build an open, emotionally fulfilling relationship with another—you must let go of the posture of independence. No one can find love by pretending to be entirely satisfied with the single life. You can convey that you're happy; there's nothing wrong with that. Just don't pretend you're not looking.[7]

If I had to come up with one word that captures the essence of protracted singleness in those who desire marriage, it would be *longing*. Proverbs 13:12 NIV tells us,

> Hope deferred makes the heart sick,
> but a longing fulfilled is a tree of life.

Here's hoping (and praying) that all your longing will lead to honest *looking,* and that in looking you will find lasting love.

NOTES

Chapter 1: Why Is It So Hard to Get Married?

1. Jillian Straus, *Unhooked Generation: The Truth About Why We're Still Single* (New York: Hyperion, 2006), 2-3.
2. Ibid., 5-6.

Chapter 3: A Years-Long Drought

1. Rachel Greenwald, *Find a Husband After 35: Using What I Learned at Harvard Business School* (New York: Random House, 2003), 6.
2. Debbie Maken, "Rethinking the Gift of Singleness," *Boundless,* 2006, http://www.boundless.org/2005/articles/a0001199.cfm.
3. Ibid.
4. Ibid.
5. Jennifer Roback Morse, "Why Not Take Her for a Test Drive?" News of the Culture Wars, http://www.jennifer-roback-morse.com/articles/cohab_fast_facts.html, September 4, 2007.
6. Ibid.

Chapter 4: Singleness: A Historical Perspective

1. Debbie Maken, "Rethinking the Gift of Singleness," *Boundless,* 2006, http://www.boundless.org/2005/articles/a0001199.cfm.
2. Ibid.
3. Ibid.
4. Ibid.
5. Ibid.
6. Ibid.
7. Ibid.

Chapter 5: Why Christian Men Aren't Dating

1. Barbara Defoe Whitehead and David Popenoe, "Why Men Won't Commit: Exploring Young Men's Attitudes About Sex, Dating and Marriage," The National Marriage Project, *The State of Our Unions: The Social Health of Marriage in America* (Piscataway, NJ: Rutgers, 2002), http://marriage.rutgers.edu/Publications/SOOU/TEXTSOOU 2002.htm.
2. Barry Schwartz, *The Paradox of Choice: Why More Is Less* (New York: HarperCollins, 2004).
3. Thomas Jeffries, "Decisions, Decisions," Part 2, *Boundless,* 2006, http://www.boundless.org/2005/articles/a0001271.cfm.
4. Jillian Straus, *Unhooked Generation: The Truth About Why We're Still Single* (New York: Hyperion, 2006), quoted in Jeffries, "Decisions."

5. Ibid., p. 27.
6. Ibid., 27-28.
7. Wendy Shalit, *A Return to Modesty: Discovering the Lost Virtue* (New York: Simon & Schuster, 1999), 5.

Chapter 6: The Allure of Modesty

1. Wendy Shalit, *A Return to Modesty: Discovering the Lost Virtue* (New York: Simon & Schuster, 1999), 97.
2. Danielle Crittenden, *What Our Mothers Didn't Tell Us: How Happiness Eludes the Modern Woman* (New York: Simon & Schuster, 1999), 31.
3. Shalit, *Return to Modesty,* 171-72.
4. Ibid., 171-72.
5. Ibid., 3-4.
6. Ibid., 4.
7. Ibid., 5.

Chapter 7: Who Moved My Altar?

1. Rachel Greenwald, *Find a Husband After 35: Using What I Learned at Harvard Business School* (New York: Random House, 2003), 6-8.
2. John T. Molloy, *Why Men Marry Some Women and Not Others: The Fascinating Research That Can Land You the Husband of Your Dreams* (New York: Warner Books, 2003), xx-xxii.
3. Candice Z. Watters, "Pulling a Ruth, Part 1," *Boundless,* 2003, http://www.boundless.org/2002_2003/departments/beyond_buddies/a0000771.html.
4. Ibid.
5. Ibid.
6. Ibid.

Chapter 8: "We Want to Be Pursued, and Men Won't Step Up to the Plate!"

1. Ellen K. Rothman, *Hands and Hearts: A History of Courtship in America* (New York: Basic Books, 1984), 32.

Chapter 10: "All the Good Ones Are Taken"

1. John T. Molloy, *Why Men Marry Some Women and Not Others: The Fascinating Research That Can Land You the Husband of Your Dreams* (New York: Warner Books, 2003), 152.
2. Ibid., 50.

Chapter 11: "Men Today Are Emotionally and Spiritually Immature and Take Too Long to Grow Up"

1. Albert Mohler, "Extended Male Adolescence—the British Version," June 28, 2005, http://www.albertmohler.com/blog_read.php?id=147, September 5, 2007.
2. Lev Grossman, "Grow Up? Not so Fast," *Time,* January 16, 2005, http://www.time.com/time/magazine/article/0,9171,1018089,00.html.
3. Ibid.

4. Ibid.
5. Ibid.
6. Dr. Laura Schlessinger, *Ten Stupid Things Men Do to Mess Up Their Lives* (New York: HarperPerennial, 1998).

Chapter 12: "Men Want to Play the Field or Have Their Cake and Eat It Too"

1. Jillian Straus, *Unhooked Generation: The Truth About Why We're Still Single* (New York: Hyperion, 2006), 79.
2. Ibid., 98.
3. Ibid., 18.

Chapter 14: "Women Expect Too Much from Us (Spiritually)— Real Men Are Rough Around the Edges"

1. Jillian Straus, *Unhooked Generation: The Truth About Why We're Still Single* (New York: Hyperion, 2006), 209-19.
2. Ibid., 214.

Chapter 16: "Christian Women Don't Keep Themselves Attractive Enough, and Many Are Overweight"

1. Shaunti Feldhahn, *For Women Only: What You Need to Know About the Inner Lives of Men* (Sisters, OR: Multnomah, 2004), 157.
2. John T. Molloy, *Why Men Marry Some Women and Not Others: The Fascinating Research That Can Land You the Husband of Your Dreams* (New York: Warner Books, 2003), xxii-xxiii, 69.

Chapter 17: "We Have a Very Real Fear of Divorce"

1. Barbara Dafoe Whitehead and David Popenoe, "Life Without Children," The National Marriage Project, *The State of Our Unions: The Social Health of Marriage in America,* 2006, http://marriage.rutgers.edu/Publications/SOOU/TEXTSOOU2006.htm.
2. John T. Molloy, *Why Men Marry Some Women and Not Others: The Fascinating Research That Can Land You the Husband of Your Dreams* (New York: Warner Books, 2003), 177.
3. Jillian Straus, *Unhooked Generation: The Truth About Why We're Still Single* (New York: Hyperion, 2006), 22.

Chapter 21: The Fields Are White unto Harvest—If You Know What to Look For

1. "Not Too Late to Meet Prince Charming After All," *ABC News.com,* May 26, 2006, http://abcnews.go.com/GMA/story?id=2007889&page=1.
2. Candice Z. Watters, "Plenty of Men to Go Around, Part 1," *Boundless,* 2006, http://www.boundless.org/2005/articles/a0001325.cfm.
3. Barna Research Group, quoted in Watters, "Plenty of Men," emphasis added.
4. Ibid.
5. John T. Molloy, *Why Men Marry Some Women and Not Others: The Fascinating Research That Can Land You the Husband of Your Dreams* (New York: Warner Books, 2003), 1.

6. Ibid., 3-4.
7. Ibid., 5.
8. Ibid., 12.
9. Ibid., 13.
10. Rachel Greenwald, *Find a Husband After 35: Using What I Learned At Harvard Business School* (New York: Random House, 2003), 10.
11. Ibid.
12. Candice Z. Watters, "Finding a Husband," *Boundless,* 2003, http://www.boundless. org/2002_2003/departments/beyond_buddies/a0000796.html.
13. Molloy, *Why Men Marry,* 10.
14. Ibid., 11.
15. Watters, "Finding a Husband."
16. Ibid.
17. Ibid.
18. Ibid.
19. Candice Z. Watters, "Pulling a Ruth, Part 1," *Boundless,* 2003, http://www.boundless. org/2002_2003/departments/beyond_buddies/a0000771.html; "Pulling a Ruth, Part 2," http://www.boundless.org/2002_2003/departments/beyond_buddies/a0000782. html.
20. Ibid.
21. Watters, "Finding a Husband."
22. David Wygant, "7 Dating Ups and Downs: How to Ride the Rollercoaster," August 31, 2007, http://dating.personals.yahoo.com/singles/datingtips/24994/7-dating-ups-and-downs, September 6, 2007.

Chapter 23: Looking for Love Like a Peasant

1. Shmuley Boteach, *Dating Secrets of the Ten Commandments* (New York: Doubleday, 2000), 34.
2. Ibid., 17-18.
3. Ibid., 19.
4. Ibid., 20-21.
5. Ibid., 21-22.
6. Shmuley Boteach, *Why Can't I Fall in Love? A Twelve-Step Program* (New York: ReganBooks, 2001), 141-42.
7. Ibid., 140-42.

BIBLIOGraPHy

Boteach, Schmuley. *Dating Secrets of the Ten Commandments*. New York: Double-day, 2000.

Boteach, Schmuley. *Why Can't I Fall in Love? A Twelve-Step Program*. New York: ReganBooks, 2001.

Crittenden, Danielle. *What Our Mothers Didn't Tell Us: How Happiness Eludes the Modern Woman*. New York: Simon & Schuster, 1999.

Feldhahn, Shaunti. *For Women Only: What You Need to Know About the Inner Lives of Men*. Sisters, OR: Multnomah, 2004.

Greenwald, Rachel. *Find a Husband After 35: Using What I Learned at Harvard Business School*. New York: Random House, 2003.

Molloy, John T. *Why Men Marry Some Women and Not Others: The Fascinating Research That Can Land You the Husband of Your Dreams*. New York: Warner Books, 2003.

Rothman, Ellen K. *Hands and Hearts: A History of Courtship in America*. New York: Basic Books, 1984.

Schwartz, Barry. *The Paradox of Choice*. New York: HarperCollins, 2004.

Shalit, Wendy. *A Return to Modesty: Discovering the Lost Virtue*. New York: Simon & Schuster, 1999.

Straus, Jillian. *Unhooked Generation: The Truth About Why We're Still Single*. New York: Hyperion, 2006.